Aubrey Lackington Moore

# The Message of the Gospel

Addresses to candidates for ordination and sermons preached chiefly before the

University of Oxford

Aubrey Lackington Moore

**The Message of the Gospel**
*Addresses to candidates for ordination and sermons preached chiefly before the University of Oxford*

ISBN/EAN: 9783744745451

Printed in Europe, USA, Canada, Australia, Japan

Cover: Foto ©Lupo / pixelio.de

More available books at **www.hansebooks.com**

THE

# MESSAGE OF THE GOSPEL

*ADDRESSES TO CANDIDATES FOR ORDINATION*

*AND SERMONS PREACHED CHIEFLY*

*BEFORE THE UNIVERSITY OF OXFORD*

BY THE LATE

## AUBREY L. MOORE, M.A.

HONORARY CANON OF CHRIST CHURCH
EXAMINING CHAPLAIN TO THE LATE AND PRESENT BISHOPS OF OXFORD
FELLOW TUTOR AND DEAN OF DIVINITY OF MAGDALEN COLLEGE
AND TUTOR OF KEBLE COLLEGE, OXFORD

London

PERCIVAL AND CO.

1891

# PREFACE

THE rapid demand for a second edition of 'SOME ASPECTS OF SIN' seems to justify the publication of another Selection from the deceased writer's papers, bearing, for the most part, on subjects connected with the Christian Ministry; and delivered either to Candidates for Ordination, or in the University pulpit. As in the case of the Lenten volume, it has been deemed expedient to make as little departure as possible from the words of the original manuscript.

# CONTENTS

## II. SERMONS BEFORE THE UNIVERSITY.

(Preached to Undergraduates at S. Mary's Church, Oxford, Feb. 7, 1886.)

# I.

# ADDRESSES TO CANDIDATES
# FOR ORDINATION,

## DELIVERED AT CUDDESDON.

A

# THREE ADDRESSES ON
# THE MESSAGE OF THE GOSPEL.

## I.

## THE MESSENGER.

'For we preach not ourselves, but Christ Jesus the Lord; and ourselves your servants for Jesus' sake.'—2 COR. iv. 5.

IN the three short addresses which it is my privilege to give to you, my fellow-workers in the great cause of Christ, I propose to speak, quite simply and practically, if I can, on some of the special difficulties and dangers incident to our high calling as Ministers of Jesus Christ,—difficulties and dangers which, if we watch our own hearts, we cannot fail to notice from the very outset of our work for God. True, we are so far prepared for difficulties, nay, even see in them often a proof of the reality of our work, because in them we welcome the fulfilment of the anticipated opposition to the work of Christ's servants which the Master Himself foretold. But the difficulties and dangers that I am thinking of are rather the home-made difficulties,—those which a little more experience, a little more knowledge, a little more liberality, above all, a little more self-forgetfulness, might have removed. Perhaps the saddest and most disheartening opposition which can meet the servant of God as he enters on an untried sphere of usefulness, full of zeal, full of hope, full of high resolves to do His Master's will, is the opposition of good people, those whom, in the main, he feels to be at one with him, bound to the service of the same Lord, steadfast in the holding fast the same truths, sealed by the same Spirit, working for the same great end, and yet unable, or, as it seems, un-willing, to work with him.   They object to some detail, to something in the manner in which the message of God is delivered, or to some side of Christian teaching to which, as it seems to them, the preacher attaches too great importance.   And henceforward, on some ground which even they themselves would hold to be trivial, they determine not to oppose but to work independently of him who, in God's provi-dence, is called to minister among them.   The result is a grievous hindrance to the work which both have at heart,—often unkind feelings, jealousies and heart-burnings, and, if not an open breach, yet that uncom-fortable and uneasy relationship which prevents those who have the same end in view from joining in harmonious action.

Of course we should be wrong to assume that such a state of things is always due to some fault or error on the part of the clergyman, and still more that a clergyman, because he is a clergyman, cannot be in the wrong.   Very often, perhaps generally, these difficulties are due to a want of tact on one side or on both, a lack of that delicate perception of what is appropriate to the special circumstances, which has been called 'the eye of experience,' but which, if it is in some a great natural gift, is perhaps most often the result not so much of experience as of strong and self-denying sympathy. Now my point is to show that if we, as God's ministers, can at any cost avoid such unpleasant and hurtful friction with those committed to our charge, it is worth an effort, nay, worth the discipline of a lifetime, both for our own sake and for the sake of the work of God committed to our keeping.

I propose then in these three addresses to touch upon some of the mistakes which we, as clergy, are most liable to commit, and which in very many cases are the cause of a grievous loss of power in our work.

1. The first matter on which we shall be tempted to form a one-sided and false opinion is our true position as God's ministers.

In speaking on this great question, I shall venture to assume that there is a sacramental character to be found in every revelation from God to man,—a double nature, which, whether we call it outward and inward, visible and invisible, human and Divine, finds its climax and its justification in the Person of the God-man. It is the same in the Revelation of Nature as in the Revelation of the Gospel. There is the outward and the visible, the co-existences and sequences which the physicist loves to observe and classify ; there is the inward and the spiritual, which not only gives a meaning to the uniformities we observe but shows them to us as the voices and the expression of a Divine Presence, the heavens declaring the glory of God, and the firmament showing His handiwork,—the sun, the moon, the stars, the trees, the hills, and the plains, each answering the obstinate questionings of the human heart with the words, *Non sum Deus—Quære super nos.*[1]

And the Christian Revelation has the same double and sacramental character running through it, as though the Mystery of the Incarnation had 'instilled its own preternatural virtue and its own paradox, into all things that bear its image and derive their nature from it.'[2]  In the Church, a body of fallible men, and yet, in some superhuman way, the Body of which Christ is the Head ; in the Bible, written by men of like passions with ourselves, and yet the true Word of God ; in the Sacraments, in the Priesthood, in the inner and more secret revelation of Conscience, there is still a reflection of the same truth, the union of the Divine and the human—united, not confused.

And the importance of this far-reaching truth to our present subject is to be found in the fact, that in practice we so easily forget that, in all these derivative cases, as in the Person of Christ Himself, the human is never sublimated or transubstantiated into the Divine, nor the Divine lost because it is united with the human.  It is a wise saying of John Locke in his

---

[1] St. Aug. *Conf.* x. 6.
[2] Bishop Forbes, Preface to Arvisenet's *Memoriale Vitæ Sacerdotalis*, p. vii.

Essay, that 'God when He makes the prophet does not unmake the man.' To be put in trust with infallible truth does not make the messenger infallible. And, on the other hand, the fact that we have the treasure in earthen vessels in no way takes from, or impairs the value of, the treasure itself.

It is then the double character of God's ministers which we must keep constantly before us if we are to realise at once the dignity and the lowliness of the priesthood. Your reading of Church History will have familiarised you with the fact that heresy is generally, if not always, one-sided or exaggerated truth ; and the truth of God is to be sought, not in a compromise between opposing errors, but in the union of two different views, which are only false when taken separately. Consequently we are not surprised to find that heresies go in pairs, the one often, in its genesis, being a reaction from the other. Docetism or Arianism, Tritheism or Unitarianism, Eutychianism or Nestorianism, in more modern times Calvinism or Universalism, and so on, all bear witness to the readiness of the human mind to acquiesce in a half-truth rather than in the whole. It is the contradictions which are inherent in any communication from God to man which give rise to the intellectual difficulties of many, and the imperfect and one-sided grasp of these contradictions, even by God's ministers, which is the source of so many difficulties in our practical work. What could be more para-doxical than S. Paul's utterances about the Christian minister ? He is the minister of Christ, he is an

ambassador from the King of Kings, he is a steward
of the mysteries of God.   Nay, the Apostle shrinks
not from such words as 'I in the Person of Christ';
'We beseech you in Christ's stead'; 'Ye received me
as the angel of God, even as Christ Jesus.'   Wonderful, mysterious, ineffable greatness !   Surely such an
one   is   taken   out   of   the   roll   of   common   men,
raised   by the greatness of his office above the in-
firmities and weaknesses and the sins of other men.
Hear the same Apostle as he grasps with a master
hand the other side of the great truth : 'We preach
not ourselves, but Christ Jesus our Lord, and ourselves your servants for Jesus' sake'; 'In nothing
behind the chiefest of the Apostles, though I am
nothing.'   His high commission only brought out to
his mind more clearly his great responsibility to be
an example to the flock, to forget self, to become all
things to all men, that he might by all means save
some.   That title which so often has thinly veiled
the pride of those who fain would 'lord it over God's
heritage,' the title of *servus servorum*, is but the
recognition of that truth which S. Paul so fully
realised, that they whose high prerogative it is to
be the ministers of Christ, in their zeal for the saving
of souls, must be ready to become 'servants of all'
that they may gain the more.

Here, in the knowledge of this double, and in some
sense paradoxical, character of the minister of Christ,
we are brought face to face with the two great temp-
tations which will beset us, the two great dangers to
which as clergymen we shall necessarily be exposed.

I mean the temptation, on the one hand, to preach ourselves, to be constantly reminding people of our greatness as God's ministers, and so by degrees to adopt a defiant and (in the popular sense of the word) a dictatorial attitude, till, if we do not domineer over those committed to our charge, we at least lose that tender loving care for their souls, without which the very greatness of our office will be a constant peril. Or, on the other hand, we are so convinced of the truth that we are to be the servants of those to whom we are sent, that we forget that higher service wherein consists our greatness, and through a too great desire to please, dare to handle the Word of God deceitfully. Let me speak quite simply and plainly on these two dangers, one of which, according to the bias of disposition or education, will probably be a danger to us all our lives through.

With regard to the danger of taking a one-sided view of our *greatness*, this perhaps, in our days, is the commoner of the two. Clergy and laity are getting to understand more fully the meaning of a priesthood in its true sense, its greatness, its awful responsibility, its efficacy for good if rightly used : but on the other hand there is a hatred, and on the whole a healthy hatred, of what has won for itself the name of 'priestcraft.' It will fall to the lot of some, perhaps many, of you, to labour in places where there is yet much of the old hatred of the name of priest, and little of the earnest and real longing for a true ministry of reconciliation. The danger here is a great one. As God's servant, you dare not simply acquiesce in the prevalent view that the clergyman is a man appointed to preach twice every Sunday, and perhaps to do a little visiting among the sick, and for the rest of his time to live like other men. And yet there is danger to your own soul if you insist upon your greatness. It is so difficult to magnify our office, and so very easy to magnify ourselves; or rather it is so easy to magnify ourselves and fancy all the time that we are simply maintaining our position as God's messengers. In such surroundings, it seems as if an imperfect and one-sided view of our position was forced upon us; as if our duty to God compelled us to emphasise that truth which, for the sake of our own humility, we would gladly keep in the background. And before we know it, we shall most likely find that what we at first did from a sense of duty, we soon come to do from a sense of self-importance, shutting ourselves up, as it were, in the fortress of our priestly greatness, and looking on those to whom we are sent as insubordinate laity who sadly need the godly discipline of ancient days. And from this point the distance between priest and people widens rapidly; and the very end and object for which we were called to greatness is in danger of being lost sight of altogether. It needs much watchfulness, much earnest self-examination, much honest self-distrust, to save those who are set in such trial states as this from falling into the devil's snare. The remedy, by God's grace, is to keep constantly before us that other truth, so necessary to our soul's health, the truth that the greatness which is ours is committed to us, not for ourselves, but for others. It is a stewardship for which we must give an account, a post of greatness, yet of tremendous responsibility. In the great day of reckoning we must give an account. Then the great question which will test our lives must be heard and answered. Not, 'Hast thou magnified thy office?' 'Hast thou maintained the dignity of the priesthood?' but, 'Hast thou done that for which I appointed thee? Hast thou been what, at thy Ordination, I charged thee to be, a faithful dispenser of that which I committed unto thee? Where are those precious ones whom thou shouldest have won over? Where are the little ones whom thou shouldest have stooped to raise? Where are the ignorant and prejudiced whom, by a lowly loving walk, thou shouldest have led to greatness? In vain hast thou treasured up in a napkin that which I intrusted to thee to use for Me. Faithless steward, unworthy minister!'

2. But there is the counter danger, no less full of peril to our faithful stewardship,—the danger, I mean, of so exaggerating the truth that we are the servants of those to whom we minister, as to adapt our teaching to the taste of the many or the great, and by so doing to mutilate and mar the truth of God. Such a result is often brought about by an honest wish to conciliate, uncorrected by a clear and definite knowledge of what is essential, and what is more or less accidental, or at least accessory. The duty of adapting our message to the modes of thought and habits of those to whom we speak is of vital importance, but the danger incident to such adaptation is not slight.

There are unpleasant truths, which as God's ministers we must speak ; there are times at which to be silent would be to be false to our God and King. Our position, as clergy of the Church of England, makes the temptation to such criminal silence or such unfaithful teaching far less than it must be in many dissenting communions. There, too often, the truth that the minister is 'the servant of the people' has been pressed so far as to obscure the truth that he should be also 'God's messenger'; and the importation of political notions into the religious sphere has often served to make him little more than the nominee and deputy of the congregation. Such a view can have no place in our Church. The minister is sent to the congregation, not invited by them. His commission is from above. He is responsible to none but God, and to those who are set over him in the Church. To speak, then, or to act, as pleasing men is a temptation that will come from our own selves, rather than our position. Yet few of us I suppose there are, however little our experience of clerical work, who have not felt how very near this temptation is to us. It is so natural to wish to please, so easy to persuade ourselves that it is good for our work that men should speak well of us. And so it is ; provided that such a result be not gained by withholding God's truth, saying 'Peace, peace' when there was no peace, or taking it for granted that wealth and position and respectability are a guarantee for Christianity, which it would be bad taste to dispute. Here, as in the former case, the true corrective is to bring into prominence that side of the truth which we are tempted to ignore, to remind ourselves that while we are servants to those to whom we minister, we are also in a higher sense the servants of God, charged with a message from Him; that we must speak, not as pleasing men, but God, that trieth the heart; that we dare keep back nothing that is profitable for those to whom we are sent; that we may not shun to declare the whole counsel of God.

Well has it been said, that 'it is the fear of God which alone can make us fearless, and the fear of man that makes us cowards.' It is the ever present sense of the greatness and importance of the message which alone can guide the messenger between the dangerous extremes of self-exaltation and the love of men's applause, between defiant self-assertion on the one hand, and complaisant self-love on the other. For both these have their source deep down in love of self, while they who have loved most truly and worked most faithfully are ever those who have been conspicuous for their self-surrender. Look at the Blessed Lord Himself as He declares that He came not to be ministered unto, but to minister. Surely if any might dare—I use a homely phrase—'to stand upon his dignity,' it was the Incarnate Son of God. Yet throughout that life of love there is not one thought of self. '*Thy* Will, not Mine.' 'I came not to do My own Will, but the Will of Him that sent Me.' 'My meat is to do that Will, and finish His work.' Nay, so absorbed, as it were, is the Lord in His message of love, that He speaks as if He Himself were nothing ' The doctrine is not Mine, but His that sent Me.' The very omnipotence of Godhead is forgotten in those words of perfect self-surrender. ' The Son can do nothing of Himself, but what He seeth the Father do.'

Look again at something of the same spirit of self-surrender in the work of the great forerunner of Christ, S. John Baptist—not clothed indeed with the high commission of the Christian priesthood, but yet charged with a message, the greatness of which dwarfs to inconceivable littleness his own personality. Who art thou? ' I am the voice. Listen to the words. Think not of me. I am nothing but a herald. The Lord cometh, before Whom I must decrease.'

Look again at those whom Christ chose to be His earliest ministers. Once more, there is seen no thought of self, no desire for greatness, no seeking to please. Come glory or come shame, it is all one ; we cannot but speak the things which we have seen and heard. ' Necessity is laid upon me,' cries S. Paul, ' yea, woe is me if I preach not the gospel.'

Look for one moment to a different sphere. See the self-forgetfulness of the patient lover of scientific truth ; see how, in stern devotion to the object of his life, he is content to live and die unknown, so only his life-work may be accomplished.

Shall we, the soldiers of the Crucified, the preachers of the truth, the servants of the Lord Jesus, show less of true heroism, less of self-surrender, allowing the thought of self, however carefully disguised, to stand in the way of the work of God ? Well do those quaint

mediæval words sum up our true position : *Quid es
ergo? Nihil et omnia.* The work is God's, the commission is from God, the power to act is God's. Our
greatness is the greatness of the charge intrusted.
What is ours? Only the littleness of a simple nature,
only the weakness of a fancied strength, only the
awful responsibility of those who must give an
account of their stewardship of the truth of God.

# II

# THE MESSAGE.

'For I determined not to know anything among you, save Jesus Christ, and Him crucified.'—1 COR. ii. 2.

WHEN we pass from the messenger to the Message which he is charged to deliver, it seems at first as if here at least there could be no misconception, no danger of misunderstanding what it is we have to proclaim. There is no hesitation or ambiguity or paradox in S. Paul's summary of his own teaching: 'We preach Christ crucified, to the Jews a stumbling-block, and to the Greeks foolishness; but to them that believe, both Jews and Greeks, Christ the power of God, and the wisdom of God.' 'I determined not to know anything among you, save Jesus Christ, and Him crucified.'

Clearly it would be wrong to suppose that this preaching of Christ crucified meant the ignoring of the infinite condescension displayed in the Incarnation, or the mighty victory that was won on Easter Day, or the triumph of the ascending Lord, or the loving care for the Church shown in the gift of Whitsunday. No one could so far misunderstand S. Paul's words, at least while we have before us his own letters and the grand sermons recorded by S. Luke. We understand at once that he meant to remind the Corinthian Church how, all through, Jesus Christ and His Death had been his theme, the beginning and the end of all his teaching, that which in his own life had made all his sufferings a cause of thankfulness, as proving his oneness with his suffering Lord,—that to which in his mind all else led up, which gave unity to his preaching and unity to his actions. Yet no man like S. Paul, of the ministers of Christ, presented that great central truth in such rich variety of illustration, pressing into the service of the Crucified the words of heathen poets, the natural love of nature, the very idolatrous worship of those to whom he spoke. None so fully brings out to us the distinctive principle of Christianity as *permeation*, not *separation*,—not the setting apart of this as sacred, and that as profane, and dividing them by a fast boundary-line, but casting over all things the halo of a Christian meaning. In the athlete of the arena he saw the Christian in his training and his struggle ; in the proud pomp of a Roman triumph he recognised a far-off picture of the ascending Lord, leading captivity captive and scattering gifts to men. In the craving after wisdom he saw the misdirected longing of the soul after the Christian γνῶσις. In the many altars, many priests, many victims, whether in Jewish or heathen worship, he beheld the shadows of the true, the one Altar, the Eternal Priest, the Divine Victim. Never did he fail sternly to rebuke that which was false, judged by the doctrine of the Crucified. Never did he fail to welcome

and to gather together all the fragments of truth which
dimly and imperfectly yet imaged out the form of the
Crucified. He looked on all the flowers of earth, and
'saw the Cross upon them. To him they were all
*cruciferæ.'* [1]

Such is the Pauline model of 'evangelical' preaching
—one in its object, manifold as the many tongues of
Whitsunday in its method of presentment. There is
a growing sense of the need of imitating S. Paul
here, but we have yet much to learn. Our tendency
is to narrow down what in S. Paul's hands was 'ex-
ceeding broad.' Some think, for instance, that 'Gospel'
preaching, as it is sometimes called, can dispense with
all those emotional or intellectual accessories which
give reality and life to teaching in every other sphere.
Earnestness and zeal are supposed to compensate for
lack of study, and to carry off that which, but for the
awfulness and solemnity of the subject and the place,
would be called vapid and insipid ;—'unobjectionable
and pious dulness,' as it has been called. There is
still a puritanical view as to the preaching of the
Gospel, which is doing serious harm to both the
preacher and his people—to the preacher, in shutting
him up to a narrow circle of ideas, driving him back,
as it were, to a theory of Jewish separation, till he is
unable to see Christ crucified everywhere ; to his
people, because such a narrow view of such a great
subject must shock and offend the cultured and the
intellectual and the refined. There is no more fitness
in leaving to matters of secular interest all the

[1] See Baring-Gould, *Mystery of Suffering*, p. 6.

intelligent exposition, all the varied illustration, all the careful reasoning, than there is in giving to the devil a monopoly of good music and high art.  Of this need of versatility in the setting forth of the great central truth of Christ crucified, I shall try and speak in my next address.

There is, however, as there always is, the counter tendency, born of reaction against the narrow view of the Christian's message, and running to an even greater evil.  This is the danger of leaving the great central truth in the background, or overlaying it with details.  Especially is this a danger in an age like ours, when, as in the prophet's vision, the breath of God is passing over the dry bones of English theology : when bone is coming to bone, every part of Christian Catholic doctrine taking its place in an harmonious and symmetric whole, clothed as it were with flesh in the restored beauty of the sanctuary, and instinct with the lifegiving Presence of God.  At such a time, the caution is not unneeded that God's ministers should seek, in all things, to observe the due proportion of parts in the setting forth of God's truth, lest the great central fact be lost sight of in things which have a meaning and a value, only in so far as they point towards and lead up to that which is the message of the Christian priest.  We often hear men of the world warned that they are committing a great mistake, forgetting that the life is more than meat, and the body than raiment, and that it profits a man but little to gain the whole world and lose his own soul, and so on.  But are not we, as clergymen, continually

making a similar mistake—failing to see what is an
end in itself, and what is but a means to an end,
—making that essential which is not so, and, as a consequence, losing sight of the supreme greatness of
the real end of all our work for God, the setting forth
the evangelical truth of 'Christ and Him crucified.'

Here the Christian teacher is by no means secured
against the faults and shortcomings of teachers in
other things. I believe if we were to take, for instance, Bacon's summary of the various forms of bias,
natural or educational, which make the reception of
scientific truth difficult and its promulgation imperfect, there are few which would not be found to
have their baneful influence on those who have received and are commissioned to forthtell the truth
of God. Something in our own religious history has
stereotyped a particular view of Christianity, and
henceforward our own religious experience becomes
the type and measure of every holy life. For instance,
if we can look back to a sudden and definite break
with a sinful life, when God's grace snatched us, like
S. Augustine, as a brand from the burning, we are
tempted to preach 'conversion' as that to which every
soul must look backward or forward, on pain of being
extruded from the pale of Christianity. On the other
hand, if by God's grace our life has been what, rare as
it is, is yet the normal life of the baptized—a going
on from grace to grace; not without sins many, yet
still without any actual falling away from God,—then
we are tempted to look on the sudden conversion
as a morbid phase of the religious life, instead of a

conspicuous, if an exceptional, showing forth of the power of the Crucified.

Or our education may have inclined us to an intellectual and philosophical view of the great truth of Christ crucified. To us it is the climax of the greatest philosophy which the world has ever seen. Most helpful is it to be able so to set forth the great truth in an intellectual age. But to allow this philosophical view to dominate our teaching, will be, for the many, to obscure or distort the truth itself. The great truths of the faith, says S. Ambrose,[1] were committed, not to logicians, but to fishermen. Or if our temperament be one on which external order and beauty in worship have a great effect, serving as a real help heavenwards, we are tempted to identify these things with the great truths which they have helped us to realise, and to give them an exaggerated and unreal importance.

Or our one-sidedness will show itself in the exclusive or excessive proclaiming of favourite doctrines, especially if we have reason to suppose that they have been too much left out of sight,—the doctrine of justification by faith as against formalism and unreality, or the need of good works as a proof of faith, or the belief in a Holy Catholic Church, or the doctrine of the Presence of Christ in the Sacrament of His love, or the benefit of Confession : all good and right so long as they point towards their true end, and do not lead

---

[1] *De Fide*, i. 13 : Non creditur philosophis, creditur piscatoribus ; non creditur dialecticis, creditur publicanis.

us to forget that our work is to preach Jesus Christ
and Him crucified.

The keeping of these truths in their true relation to
the central truth is perhaps one of the hardest
practical difficulties in our teaching.   Different minds
will doubtless approach the truth of Christ by
different avenues, and it is the part of the Christian
teacher to keep all these avenues open ; not to close
this one or that, because to his own feelings or disposition it has few attractions ; nor to mark one as
the normal and orthodox, and the rest as 'lawful but
not expedient.'   We are most of us far too ready with
our Acts of Uniformity, our tests and home-made
criteria of what is good and true, forgetting often,—in
our zeal for this view or that of what, on any showing, is a means and not an end,—the end to which,
by the wondrous working of God's Holy Spirit, both
alike may lead.

This keeping ever before us the essential and the
eternal, and for the rest, not ignoring it, but keeping it
in its due relation of subordination, seems to have
been included in that advice to S. Timothy : 'Study to
show thyself approved of God, a workman that needeth
not to be ashamed, rightly dividing (ὀρθοτομοῦντα) the
word of truth.'   This ὀρθοτομία is that which made
S. Paul's own teaching so wonderfully varied and yet
so evangelical.   All through it there was the realising
of the great truth as a fact in his own life, the intense
personal appropriation, if we may use the word, of a
personal Saviour 'Who loved me, and gave Himself for
me.'   Everything else was lighted up by that truth, and

served to bring out in all its rich variety the preaching of Jesus Christ and Him crucified. All other truths owed their greatness to their relation to this, but as compared with that truth itself all others were transient, not eternal—means, and not ends.

Lift up your eyes for one moment to that picture of heavenly worship as it is given in the Revelation of S. John. There, in that eternal state where Church and Creed and Sacraments and Bible are precious only for what they have been, one central Object is still unchanged, the One Object Which shall rivet the gaze of angels and archangels and all the company of heaven, and it is a Lamb as it had been slain. Oh! it is not the might nor the majesty, not the ineffable glory of the King of the Ages on which the redeemed shall love to gaze. There is a sight more wondrous far, a mystery which angels desire to look into, before which men bow in ever-growing thankfulness and awe,—the mystery of the God-man slain for man, bearing still on the Throne of His Glory the marks of His transcendent love, even the mystery which on earth we were charged to proclaim when we were sent to preach Jesus Christ and Him crucified.

I think it is the keeping of all the parts of Christian truth in due connection with and subordination to the central truth that makes some High Churchmen so 'evangelical.' People expect to hear them talk of nothing but the Church and the Priesthood and the Sacraments, and they find that there is one subject which towers above all, and gives life to all. First, and before all, or rather in and through all, they

preach Christ, that is Apostolic preaching,—for the
first Christians, it has been said, did not believe in
Christianity, they believed in *Christ*.

Do not be ashamed of that word 'evangelical,' or
allow it to degenerate into a party name.  It is your
privilege, my brothers, to prepare yourselves here for
the preaching of Christ.  Your preaching must be
*evangelical*, or you will be false to your trust.  But
there is a change coming over the thought of the day
as to what 'Gospel' preaching is, and it is a move in
the direction of a fuller appreciation of truth.  Even
in days which some of us can remember, a Gospel
sermon was one which included the whole of what
used to be called the scheme or plan of salvation.  If
it was not this, it savoured of worldly wisdom.  And so
much used to be said of 'the foolishness of preaching' as
an instrument in God's hand, that the result was often
'the preaching of foolishness.'  Meanwhile there had
crept into this so-called plan of salvation a heathen
view of propitiation, and a legal fiction borrowed from
the law-courts which was profoundly immoral.  Now
we are unlearning this.  We preach the Atonement in
the light of the Incarnation, not the Incarnation as a
step to the Atonement.  People who read neither
S. Thomas nor Duns Scotus will say this is a revival
of Scotism.  Others will say it is a substitution of
theological for an evangelical preaching.  Others,
with more truth, will point to it as an appeal from
Augustinian to Athanasian theology.  But none of
these is exactly true.  We preach Christ crucified.
If the centre of gravity seems to have shifted from

the Atonement to the Incarnation, it is only because the Atonement, amid the false theories of a degenerate age, had lost its true meaning, and had come to be set over against the Incarnation.

The priest's message always and everywhere is the Gospel of reconciliation, the priest's work is to bring souls back to God by the power of Christ's finished work. And Church and Priesthood and Sacraments are the means which Infinite Love has ordained for that end. Teach the whole truth as S. Paul did, but keep the proportion of the faith, and always and in all preach Christ.

# III

# THE MODE OF DELIVERY.

## CHRISTIAN VERSATILITY.

'I am made all things to all men, that I might by all means save some.
And this I do for the Gospel's sake, that I might be partaker
thereof with you.'—1 COR. ix. 22, 23.

WHEN God the Holy Spirit descended on the
waiting Church at Whitsunday, He revealed Himself as one and many, one in His Eternal Nature,
manifold in His varied operations. The curse of
Babel is revoked at Pentecost. The many tongues
of man's self-will had brought confusion, now the
Spirit of God has given peace. The many tongues
are consecrated now, consecrated to the work of God,
inspired by the Holy Ghost to the duty of telling
forth to every kingdom, and nation, and language,
the wonderful works of God. That old motto, so
familiar to most of us: 'Many are the tongues of
men, but God's is ever one,'[1] may, in the light of
Whitsuntide, be just reversed. It is God's Spirit Who
speaks in many tongues and works by many means,
while man in his impotence can understand and use
but one. Yet, in proportion as the life of God's

[1] πολλαὶ μὲν θνητοῖς γλῶσσαι, μία δ' ἀθανάτοισι.

minister is guided by that self-same Spirit, he too will learn to speak the unchanging truth in varied ways as the Spirit gives him utterance.

This is the thought I want to leave with you—*the need of a Christian versatility* in our personal and pastoral relations with those for whose souls we must give account. 'I am made all things to all men, that I might by all means save some.' And let us think of this grace of character not as a natural gift, except to a few, but as something to be striven after, something to be prayed for, something worth the discipline of a life, because of the power which is given us thereby to proclaim the wonderful works of God.

The need of this grace is evident when we remember that that same tendency to narrowness which hampers the messenger in the delivery of the message is also a constant difficulty to the hearer in receiving the message. And unless, as God's ministers, we can by our own many-sidedness meet the one-sidedness of others, they may be for ever repelled from the truth which we have in trust.

One of the most fruitful causes of failure in ministerial work, or of what we call failure, however in God's providence it may be overruled for good, is that we do not understand our people. We and they, or we and some of them, move as it were in different planes. Our thoughts and feelings run on different lines, and clearly till we can at least in part overcome this difference, our teaching will be in 'a tongue not understanded of the people.'

For instance, to take such cases as will meet us at

the outset :—There are few things more shocking to a cultured, a sensitive, and reverent nature, than the rough and rude way in which the uneducated will speak of sacred things. We are tempted to preach a crusade against it as profane and wicked, and it is some time before we come to see that again and again the fault is more in the expression than the feeling ;—that a delicate sense of sin and a real know-ledge of the holiness of God often underlie what at first we put down as unseemly familiarity with holy things. Or, again, we are too young to have a natural sympathy with the old and feeble ; or too old to enter into the pleasures of the young ; or too bright and cheerful to be quite at one with the gloomy type of religion which some have stamped as orthodox ; too lax for some, too rigid for others ; not intel-lectual enough for these, nor practical enough for those. And our English want of elasticity, on which we often foolishly pride ourselves, serves to stereo-type, and even to justify, these faults. Yet faults they are, and to be striven and prayed against, if we would not curtail and limit the sphere of usefulness which God has appointed for us. Very few of us are naturally gifted with those qualifications which enable men to move freely in the thoughts of others. To most of us, it is an effort, and an effort which is only possible under the power of strong and earnest sympathy guided by the Spirit of God.

' All things to all men '—meeting men on their own ground, sympathising with them in their favourite pursuits, showing as far as we can an intelligent interest in their trade or profession, joining the young in their games, giving a helping hand to those who are just entering on that which is to be their work in life, showing, as far as may be, sympathy with sorrows which as yet we have not felt, moving in society as those who feel no time lost in the service of their Lord which teaches them more of the feelings and habits of thought of those to whom they have to speak. We must learn their language if we are to make them understand us. We have got to claim all things for Christ, to see every new truth as a revelation of Him Who is the Truth, to leave no region of human activity or human thought outside. Especially in this day must we do what we can, according to the powers which God has given us, to keep abreast of the intellectual and scientific progress of our time. In the days when, at least in country parishes, the parson was the only man of education, it mattered less if his education had been rudely cut short at the time of his degree; but now, when not only the educated classes, so called, but the intelligent working man, may justly look down on a man who is a ' divine, and nothing but a divine,' or when those whom we were sent to guide are compelled to say or think of us, ' He cannot help me, good as he is, for he cannot understand me,'—when I say such a state of things is not only possible, but of common occurrence, it is imperative upon us, who are called to be teachers of others, to relax no effort in teaching ourselves.

We hear much of intellectual difficulties. How many of us attempt to qualify ourselves, I do not

say to answer them, but even to understand them ?
Again and again grievous harm is done to those for
whom, as for us, Christ died, by the way in which
those who have never themselves experienced difficulties of belief put such things aside as the work of
the devil, or as a wilful carping at revealed truth.   It
is for us, as God's ministers, to find what it is which
each soul needs, and by a tender sympathy with
that need to adapt (I use the term advisedly) the
great central truth, or rather show how it adapts itself,
to that need.   In one the craving for a God of love
will be predominant, in another the exigencies of
Divine justice will be the starting-point of his theology.
To fail to throw ourselves into the different mental
and moral states of our people will be to fail to
deliver our message aright.   As far as we may dare
to forecast character John Stuart Mill, the 'atheist,'
as some call him, might have been a loving member
of Christ's Holy Church if when he asked for bread
he had not been given a stone, when he was yearning
for a God of love he had been taught Christianity
instead of Calvinism, and God had been presented to
him as He is, instead of as a great Executioner.

  'Versatility' or many-sidedness in intellectual
matters is no doubt harder and needs more discipline
than versatility in other matters.   A clergyman who
is earnest in his work, anxious to omit nothing which
will conduce to the great end, will very soon learn to
appreciate the need of versatility in his ordinary life.
Things, little in themselves, become great when the
Holy Spirit consecrates them to the service of

Christ. Again and again the friendly intercourse which began on the cricket-field or in the drawing-room becomes, by God's grace, a παιδαγωγὸς bringing to the school of Christ those who had little liking or reverence for 'parsons' or 'preaching.' So subtle are the threads which bind us to those committed to our charge that we dare not put aside any means of influence which is given to us. Natural gifts, accomplishments, a genial and kindly disposition, may all be made the organs of God's Holy Spirit. 'In the morning sow thy seed, in the evening withhold not thy hand ; for thou knowest not whether shall prosper, either this or that, or whether they both shall be alike good.' It is for us to sow beside all waters, trusting to God Himself, as He will, and when He will, to give the increase.

Such a versatility, intellectual and social, will have many enemies. Puritanism will rise up against it with stern and vigorous denunciations :—It is a dangerous and unwise, if not dishonest, parleying with the enemy ; it is Jesuitism, which justifies the means by the end ; to adapt God's truth is to misrepresent it ; to live in the world is to be of the world ; and so on.

Such is the vigorous, even if narrow-minded, protest against what of course is a real danger. Only here, as elsewhere, to be forewarned is to be forearmed. What we have to be on our guard against is not the versatility itself, but a wrong motive, or the absence of a good one to direct it. This is well illustrated by the different forms which versatility took in the history of the Greeks. In the age of Pericles it was the great Hellenic virtue, on the excellence of which the Greek prided himself. 'It was a happy and graceful flexibility.' Freedom from prejudice, freedom from stiffness, openness of mind, amiability of manners, clearness and propriety of language,—all these seem to have had their part in that which enabled the Athenian, without loss of earnestness or 'relaxation of moral force,' to become all things to all men. In the age of Aristotle this versatility is still a grace, but a subordinate grace, of character. It is now little more than an elegant accomplishment, which the Athenian gentleman, enveloped in a sense of dignity and self-importance, only cultivated that he may avoid the unpleasant extremes of buffoonery and boorishness. Four hundred years later the same word appears in the Epistle of S. Paul to the Ephesians, and lo, it is coupled with filthiness and foolish talking ; it is the 'jesting' which is not convenient. And yet S. Paul was remarkable for the possession of εὐτραπελία in its highest and noblest sense. Wherein then does the flexibility of S. Paul differ from the frivolity and fickleness of the Ionians of Asia Minor? Simply and solely in the motive which actuated him. It was when Greece lost its reality, its earnestness, when its moral fibre became relaxed, that this grace of character became hateful and contemptible. With S. Paul there was an ever-present purpose. 'I am made all things to all men, that I might by all means save some.' It was the intense earnestness of one who had a message of salvation to deliver, the strong and vivid sense of a Divine commission resting on him which made S. Paul's flexibility a model for the Christian minister in all ages. 'This I do for the Gospel's sake, that I might be partaker thereof with you.' It is this principle which must guide us through the endless complexities of a life in the world. Nothing is common or unclean, if it can be made subservient to the great end of bringing souls to God. If some father in Christ of rich experience in such matters were to give us a system of rules, deciding what is lawful, and what is unlawful,—when flexibility and versatility is good, and what its limits,—he would have furnished us only with a casuistical treatise, suggesting as many difficulties as it solves. For the limits of versatility depend on its usefulness in helping on the work we have at heart, and this usefulness must depend in a large measure on the local and accidental circumstances of those amongst whom we labour.

Generally speaking, we may say that to preach Christ crucified without that power of adaptation of which S. Paul is such a notable example, is to circumscribe and limit the sphere of work which God has mapped out for us. While, on the other hand, to cultivate versatility without the earnestness and singleness of purpose of one who has a message from God to deliver, is to prove ourselves unfaithful stewards of the mysteries of God.

One concrete example is worth many abstract statements, and in speaking of the need of Christian versatility in the work of God, I can think of no

C

better illustration than that afforded by the different characters of Gregory the Great and the missionary S. Augustine. Both were earnest, both enthusiastic, both ready to spend and to be spent, if only they might preach Christ crucified to the rude barbarians of Anglo-Saxon England. But S. Augustine from first to last was hampered by a want of elasticity, a narrowness, intellectual rather than moral, which led him to identify Christianity with that form of it with which, in his convent life at Rome, he had been familiar. S. Gregory, with that wisdom which a knowledge of many men and many minds had given, a delicate sense of the difference between essential and accidental, above all with a conviction of the necessity of what I have called 'adaptation' in the preaching of Christianity, stands out as a model of wide and liberal-minded earnestness. When the collision with the old British Church came, S. Augustine with the same want of flexibility, not unmixed perhaps with a sense of his own importance as Metropolitan of England, was ready to contend to the last about the wording of a Liturgy, or the form of a tonsure, or the style of chronology. In vain S. Gregory's wise warning that he should adapt himself to national customs as far as possible, and 'not value things because of places, but places for the good things they contained.' With all his earnestness and missionary zeal, S. Augustine's want of versatility in the delivery of his message narrowed down his success to a small portion of the east of England, leaving the rest to be evangelised by the remnants of that very British Church with whom he would not work.

Over and over again we clergy make the same mistake, losing the co-operation of good and earnest men, because in some detail they 'follow not us.' Over and over again the narrowness which is born of ignorance or pride loses us the opportunity of speaking God's message of salvation to the souls whom God has sent us to call.

Dear brethren, in the hours that yet remain before your Ordination, will you not pray for a double measure of the Holy Spirit's gifts, the fire of a Divine and self-forgetting love, the power which shall enable you to preach.the truth of Christ in all its fulness and variety, the many tongues of Pentecost that you may speak to every soul in the language that it knows, so that in the day of Christ ye may rejoice that ye 'have not run in vain, nor laboured in vain'?

# IV.

## VOCATION FOR THE MINISTRY.

THE first question which is asked in the Ordination Service, whether of a Deacon or a Priest, is one which concerns Vocation for the special work of the Ministry. The form of the question differs slightly in the two cases, and for reasons which lie on the surface. You who are to be admitted to the office of Deacon will be asked, 'Do you trust that you are inwardly moved by the Holy Ghost to take upon you this Office and Ministration, to serve God for the promoting of His glory, and the edifying of His people?' And your answer must be, 'I trust so.' For you, on the other hand, who are to be admitted to the Priesthood, the question will take a more definite form. Instead of 'Do you trust that you are inwardly moved?' you will be asked, 'Do you think in your heart, that you be truly called, according to the will of our Lord Jesus Christ, and the order of this Church of England, to the Order and Ministry of Priesthood?' And the answer should be, 'I think it.' The difference in the two forms seems to imply, that the Diaconate, though not a probation in the sense that we are at liberty, if we find ourselves unfit for the work, to return to the ordinary life of a layman, is yet a real probation, a time in which we may make actual trial of ourselves and of our purpose, and see how far that 'trust' which we expressed on our entry into the ministry is well grounded ; not a mere impulse, however real at the time it may have seemed, but a true call from God to a devoted life.

Thus the matter of Vocation is one of vital importance to candidates for Holy Orders. What is to justify them in their 'trust,' that in seeking the sacred ministry they were moved by the Holy Ghost? By what tests are they to try themselves and their work during their Diaconate, that, when they present themselves for the higher order of Priesthood, they may 'think in their heart that they are truly called'? It is clear that such questions must be answered not by *feelings* only but by *facts*. It does not need much self-knowledge to teach us that our feelings, as we commonly understand that word, are no safe guide in this matter, any more than in that great change of heart and life which we call conversion. They offer us no certain standard. Those who trust their feelings alone are as often wrong as those whose distrust of their feelings leads them to fall into the opposite error. A feeling is not always right, and it certainly is not always wrong. A very slight experience of pastoral work is sure to bring us into relation with those whose confident, even exultant, feeling that they are saved is no sure evidence to set against their lives, while others we shall see living the saintly life,

and yet in God's providence never suffered to know
the joy of His salvation.

We must put aside mere feeling then as a standard, however often the 'inward call' has been based
upon it.

More than that, if we are to deal with this question
aright, we must certainly put on one side those
interested motives which so often make the question
of vocation hard for earnest men; while those who are
not in earnest are in danger of putting out of sight
the real question altogether.  I am not thinking so
much of the baser motives which, in times gone by,
have ruined many a life, and which exist as a rare
survival in our day,—such as the family living, or the
prospect of rapid preferment, or the desire at all cost
to retain a clerical fellowship.  I am thinking rather
of motives which may and should rightly have their
weight and place, though not the chief place,—the
earnest wish of a father to see his son dedicate his
life to the highest of all earthly callings, or the prospect of enlarged influence for good, or the consciousness of special gifts which may be consecrated to the
service of God.  To those who are really in earnest,
these considerations seriously complicate the question
of Vocation.  From mere honesty and simplicity of
purpose, we distrust ourselves.  To have been brought
up in a clerical atmosphere, to have gone through
boyhood and manhood with the consciousness that
those who are dearest to us want us to be 'clergymen,'
still more perhaps to know that we have ability and
power of influence, or the gift of eloquence,—all these

things make the question of Vocation difficult. We are afraid of being unconsciously biassed; and the very working of God's grace in our immediate surroundings, or in the qualifications He has given us, leads us to distrust ourselves. We want then to steer our course between a scrupulousness which has become morbid, and a carelessness which will accept anything or nothing as a call from God.

Perhaps it will help us in this matter if we think of the record left to us by two men in whom the thought of ' Vocation ' was a very present power, and who have told us something of the steps by which they realised the truth.

In the sixth chapter of his Prophecy you will find the story of Isaiah's call. ' In the year that king Uzziah died,' he says, as though he loved to trace back to a definite point in time the beginning of his prophetic labours, ' I saw the Lord sitting on His Throne.' He saw the glory of the heavenly world, he saw the six-winged angels and heard their song of praise. And the first thought was ' Woe is me! for I am undone; because I am a man of unclean lips.' Then came the messenger with a live coal from the altar to touch his lips and purge his sin. Then he heard the voice, ' Whom shall I send, and who will go for us?' And the prophet answered, ' Here am I; send me.' Notice the order of the vision : the presence of God and the sense of sin ; the consciousness of pardon and the readiness to answer to God's call.

Now turn from the Old Testament to the New, and read the account of S. Paul's conversion as he

records it, or as it is recorded by his friend S. Luke.
We are as anxious to reject, as a previous age was to
discover,—a sudden break in the continuity of life.
We do not speak of conversion as our fathers did,
and yet we know that there are in every life certain
definite turning-points, determined often by causes
external to the man,—awful moments of choice, when,
for good or ill, a tremendous impulse is given to the
soul's life. Such a turning-point was the conversion
of S. Paul. 'When did the conversion take place?'
people have asked. 'Was it at the moment when he
fell to the ground, and for the first time heard the
voice of Jesus Whom he persecuted? Or was it when
he offered himself up to the new Master in the words,
" Lord, what wilt Thou have me to do?" Or was his
conversion a more gradual thing, extending over those
three days of darkness, when the eye, closed to the
external world, turned in upon itself, and saw all
things transformed by the light which shone upon
the road? Or was the conversion incomplete?—the
unrenewed nature wrestling, still unwilling to yield
to God till the moment when, among the angels who
watched the conflict, the cry was heard, " Behold he
prayeth "?' We are not careful to answer these
questions. We cannot pierce the mystery of the
Spirit's working in the soul, or reduce it to a formula.
Enough that the turning-point in that life which
stands out with such marked individuality on the
page of the Bible was reached when Saul the per-
secutor had realised the truth that he was 'a chosen
vessel'; that there was a special place and duty

assigned to him in the economy of God's world, and that to seek for ought outside and beyond this was a vain 'kicking against the goad.'

Compare together step by step the call of Isaiah and the conversion of S. Paul, and you will find points of difference, no doubt, but one characteristic you will find prominent in both,—the realising of the fact that God had a special work for them to do, a work for which indeed neither felt that he was worthy, and yet a work which each was impelled to do, because in God's ordering they were the 'chosen vessels.' They had realised the meaning of ' Vocation.'

Now nothing is more common than the phrase 'choosing a vocation.' We hear it every day. Examine the phrase, and you will see that it is a contradiction in terms. Vocation, or, as we say sometimes, a man's calling in life, can mean nothing more nor less, to any one who believes in God, than the special work to which He calls each one of us. In some sense, no doubt, we can choose this or reject it. But if we reject it, and choose something else, we do not choose another vocation, though popular language may justify such a phrase,—we choose that which is not our vocation. In other words, we sacrifice our lives in a vain kicking against the goad. What a world of sadness and disappointment and misery is often covered by those words we use so lightly, when we speak of a man having 'mistaken his vocation'! If it means anything more than the superficial remark that he might have been in another line more successful, as the world counts success, does it not mean that God's purpose in that life has been frustrated, that God's call was never obeyed, that the work, the true work of life, was never done, that the talent which the Master put in trust was never used, and that all the life has been a struggle against God's will, that is, against man's own true good? Saddened lives, soured lives, disappointed lives, weary lives, wasted lives, lives dissipated in undirected or misdirected efforts, lives that by a natural transition have exchanged the 'unchartered freedom' of which once they boasted for the merest slavery to accidental and external circumstances—how common are all those! We wonder that there is so much unhappiness in a world which its Creator pronounced to be 'very good.' But does not it all work back to that one word 'vocation,' and do not happiness and wretchedness mainly follow the distinction which separates the lives of those who have found, and those who have missed their true vocation?

'Our whole predestination,' says Bourdaloue, 'well-nigh turns on the choice we make of our condition of life. Thereon depends almost exclusively the happiness or misery of our eternity.' Our life-work is mapped out for us in the purposes of God. He is waiting to show us what it is. On God's side predestination is 'a certain enchaining of graces prepared for us.' These graces we may refuse or accept. But every grace given and received is a limiting of that false freedom which is man's ruin. Holy Baptism separates us to the kingdom of God. Every secret operation of the Holy Spirit upon our lives seals us to a more

special purpose within that sphere. Some are called
to the Sacred Ministry, some to the hardly less im-
portant work of the Christian layman. Vocation is
for all, special vocation to the Ministry only for a few.
S. Paul loved to look back to that separating power
of God's Holy Spirit, and see it in his whole life. He
was separated from his mother's womb, set apart as a
member of that narrow sect of religionists whose
watchword was 'separation.' But a new meaning was
to be read into that word, a meaning which only
became clear at his conversion. He was separated
unto the Gospel ἀφωρισμένος εἰς εὐαγγέλιον; and once
more it was by the special action of that same Spirit
that he with S. Barnabas was 'separated' for the missionary work. Hence it was that the word ἀφορισμός
came to be used as a synonym for Ordination. It was
the outward and visible counterpart of the inward
and spiritual call.

Something of this consciousness of separation and
setting apart by God for His work ought surely to be
present to those who trust that they are moved by the
Holy Ghost; and still more to those who, in the
presence of God and the Congregation, declare that
they think in their heart that they are truly called to
the priesthood. If so it will show itself and make its
presence known. The life for which we believe we
are chosen of God will not present itself to us as one
amongst the many lives which, if circumstances had
been different, we might have chosen. We shall not
simply feel a preference for the clerical life, as that
one which, after due balancing of *pros* and *cons*, seems

to us the best, still less as the life which, under the circumstances, is to be desired. If we let such considerations decide us, we have not realised what 'vocation' means. The consciousness that we are chosen by God to this work lifts us out of the region of individual feeling into the sphere of the necessary and the universal. It is no longer, 'I would rather be a clergyman than enter any other profession I know of,' but, 'I must be a clergyman whatever happens.' 'I cannot but speak.' 'Necessity is laid upon me ; yea, woe is me if I preach not the Gospel.' 'My object in life is to apprehend that for which also I am apprehended.' It is like the difference between regulating conduct by considerations of interest and expediency, and being in all things guided by duty. It is a mere commonplace of moral science to say that while we are trusting ourselves to utilitarian considerations, we are moving in the sphere of the contingent, and the variable, and the unknown. We are never sure that we have estimated the chances rightly. But the consciousness of duty makes us in a moment independent of such considerations. We are prepared at all risks to do what we know is right, or rather we feel that there is *no* risk in doing what is our duty. So it is with 'Vocation.' If we have to choose, we dare not decide ; if our work is chosen for us, we dare not hesitate.

I do not of course mean that all feel and must feel their vocation in the same degree, any more than all feel the force of what has been called the 'categorical imperative' in morals ; but this I believe—something of

the '*I must*' will be present to all who realise Vocation.
According to the degree of our communion with God
will be the clearness with which we shall hear Him
saying to us, 'Ye have not chosen Me, but I have
chosen you.' For the rest I may dare to shift the
responsibility to God. He has called me to the work ;
He will give me strength to do the work.

# V

# THE THOUGHT OF VOCATION THE SOURCE OF STRENGTH IN THE PRIESTLY LIFE.

THE thought of Vocation which is brought before us, on our entry into Holy Orders, will be, if it be realised at all, a present power all our lives through; influencing our work in ways that we hardly think of, and lifting us up above the littleness and imperfections of our human nature. This is the subject I want you to think of now. How will the consciousness that we are truly called to the Sacred Ministry help us in our after work?

And, first, I think it will help us by making our work really *clerical.* The consciousness that we are sent by God to deliver His message, called and separated that we may deliver it, will, I believe, save us, as nothing else will, from gradually slipping into a way of living which has nothing distinctly clerical about it. I do not mean that we should give up preaching sermons and talking about matters of the greatest moment, but that if we have not realised what Vocation is, we shall be in danger of gradually, and to ourselves imperceptibly, adopting a life which, though it may still be that of a Churchman, is not definitely that of a Priest. I am thinking specially, and you will not wonder that such thoughts should come into my mind,—I am thinking specially of those who are called, as some of us are, to Academical work,—not because we happen to hold clerical fellowships, but because we honestly believe that the University is the sphere in which we are called to labour as Priests of God. I should be the last to underrate the difficulties of such a vocation. But no one who knows the vital importance, in such a transition time as ours, of having those engaged in University work who believe that God has called them to be His ministers, would dare, because of these difficulties, to shrink from the work. That all those who are called by God to a direct and ministerial dealing with souls should be extruded from our Universities that they may give themselves to parochial work, must seem, to any one who still believes in our Universities as places of education, a suicidal policy. We want more men who will dedicate and consecrate their Academical work, accepting it as the sphere in which they are to realise their vocation. The opportunities for doing this, and the ways in which it may be done, must differ in different Colleges. Much will be thrown upon tact and judgment and sympathy. But the difference between those who have realised and those who have not realised their vocation to the ministry must show itself. Times have changed since the Colleges were thought of as monastic, or at least clerical, bodies. But the fact that a College

Fellowship is still accepted as a title for Holy Orders ought to indicate to us that we are intended to find a real cure of souls in the College to which we are attached. 'Clerical work,' as it is called, in vacation, and occasional sermons in term time, may be helpful to us, but will not satisfy those who know what Vocation means. As Priests (whether in the parish or in Academical work) we are called to deal with souls. And those who have realised this, if they are engaged in College teaching, will seek to find their work not outside of, but in and through their ordinary College duties. Can we deal with undergraduates as if we were not only tutors, but clergy? I, for one, believe we can, and that, not only will they be grateful to us for it, but that, in their heart of hearts, they will think we have failed in our duty if we do not. I remember very well—it is a small matter, but it will illustrate my meaning,—I remember very well what the effect was upon me and others when we were boys at school, when the class master, who was a clergyman, and who had till then done nothing but teach us Latin and Greek, told us one day that he had been thinking about things, and had come to the conclusion that, as a clergyman, as well as a school-master, he had a special duty towards us, and there-fore he intended, one day in every week, before the ordinary work began, to say a few words to us as a clergyman. I don't know that his method was a very good one. Boys are not fond of sermons. But I believe there was not one boy in his class who did not respect him and honour him for daring, in defiance of school traditions, to do that duty to which God had called him. Undergraduates need direction and real spiritual sympathy, much more than many people think : and we are not flaunting sacerdotalism in their faces if we try to keep before them and ourselves the truth that we are 'called to the Ministry.' At all events, and this is my main point, if we have at all realised what Vocation means, we shall be willing to risk the chance of being misunderstood, rather than allow our clerical character to be subsumed in that of the College tutor.

*Mutatis mutandis*, the same is true for those who are called to the work of the Holy Ministry as masters in schools. Here, however, the transition from the secular to the religious is often made easy by the fact that the clerical masters are often intrusted with the preparation of their pupils for Confirmation. That such work often falls to the lot of those who are not yet in Priest's Orders is an anomaly, which no one feels more keenly than the Deacons themselves ; but at least it makes it easier for them to deal with those intrusted to them, not merely as pupils, but as those whose soul's life is committed to their charge.

In the ordinary work of a parish it would seem at first as if there was no danger of a clergyman for-getting the work to which he is called. But even here, without the consciousness of real vocation going with us, it is almost impossible that we should not make a line of demarcation between sacred and secular, which, if it does not go so far as to make us put aside our clerical character with our surplice, at least makes it hard, if not impossible, for us to pass from the easy social call to a real pastoral visit. Especially is this the case in the visits which we pay to those who are our equals in the social scale. How are we to break through the hard crust of politeness and speak to the real self? How many a parish visit must we of necessity feel to have been simply waste of time, so far as concerns our real work, our real vocation! We cannot afford to despise anything, however secular it may seem, which really brings us nearer to our people, but to use that nearness as one who realises his vocation would wish to use it, is in truth no easy matter. And so, instead, we go on waiting for an opportunity,—hoping that we may be called in, in sickness or trouble, and be able to say what we have in our hearts, and perhaps all the time those that we are visiting are longing for us to throw aside the cloak of politeness and speak to them as God's ministers. If, as we think, many dissenting Christians make the mistake of speaking out of season, I am sure many Churchmen err on the other side. We are so much afraid of doing anything in bad taste that we are often content to put on one side the message from God with which we are charged.

It is the consciousness of Vocation which alone can make our lives really *clerical*; but this is not all. It is the same conviction that we are chosen by God for the work which lifts us up above the common anxieties as to success or failure. As we realise in our lives what it is to work for God, we seem to attain to something of *a 'holy indifference' as to results.*

Whether men will hear, or whether they will forbear,
we must speak. And '*I must*' here, as in the moral
sphere, implies '*I can.*' We do not however learn
this in a moment. Our first thought is about ourselves and our unfitness for the great work. 'Who
am I, that I should go?'[1] 'Lord, I am not eloquent.'[2]
Till we realise what Vocation means, we think of what
we are going to do for God, instead of thinking what
He is going to do by us. And the result is very
often disappointment and weariness. Our first impulse has worn itself out, and if we go on with our
work it is in a dull, lifeless, routine fashion. We
have no more heart in it, and our people soon find it
out. And yet we began with such earnest self-
devotion : we meant to do God's work, and we ex-
pected great results—at least we thought people
would understand that we were engaged in well-
doing. But things did not go as we hoped. There
was little visible result. Those we thought we were
leading to God broke away, and all our efforts seemed
wasted. And then, worse than want of hoped-for
success, we found our very motives challenged or
misunderstood. We thought, like Moses, that people
would have understood that we were the chosen
deliverer, and we are shocked and disheartened that
those we are trying to help turn round upon us and
say, 'Who made thee a ruler and a judge over
us?' And the disappointment and weariness when
it comes is generally great in proportion to the zeal
with which the work was begun. For, perhaps, what

1 Exod. iii. 11.　　　　2 Exod. iv. 10.

we thought zeal covered a good deal of self-confidence, and God would have us know that it is He
Who works, not we. At all events, visible success is
no trustworthy test. The promise is certain; the
time is left in God's hands. 'In due season we shall
reap, if we faint not,' but the due time is God's, not
ours. The moment we begin to ask ourselves—and
which of us has not done so ?—'Am I doing any good ?
Had I not better give up the effort and confess that
I have failed?' we may be quite sure that we are
bringing in human tests of heavenly work. Some
one has compared our undertaking and purposes to
that great image which Nebuchadnezzar saw in his
dream. The head was of fine gold, so are the beginnings of most men's plans. Nothing is too costly, no
labour too great. The breast and the arms are of
silver. Interest begins to slacken. Our views of
possible success are modified. We have less exalted
notions of what we are going to do. Lower still, the
silver has become brass, bright as the golden head,
but not real, not genuine. We go on with our work,
and it looks the same; but it is brass, not gold. The
feet are part iron and part clay. Dreary ending to a
work so nobly begun ! What a picture of imperfection
a gradual deterioration—gold first, clay last ! Such is
the spiritual history of many who did run well ; such
is the work of many who started with high purposes
to labour for God. Now they are jaded, cold, half-
hearted. 'Weary in well-doing' sums up their
interior as well as their exterior life.

And yet one thing might have saved them from all

this,—just the thought of Vocation, and the letting results alone. The necessity to speak, the ' I must' of one who knows that God has sent him to the work, puts out of sight the question of success or failure. He who is conscious of this may have toiled all the night and taken nothing, but there is still the command to ' let down the net.' ' I must, therefore I can '; though I seem in the very effort to fail, God has called me to work for Him, and work I must. How my feeble and often frustrated efforts can promote God's glory I cannot see. Whether in nature or in grace, we cannot judge of God's purposes 'ex analogia hominis.' In nature I can only read His Will as it is written there; in my life-work I can only labour, and listen, and obey. The impulse which is nourished on success dies when its food fails. The only lasting power in our lives is the knowledge that our meat is to do God's Will and to labour in His work.

Go forth then to your new life, strong in the consciousness of Vocation, your whole clerical life made real by it, and lifted up above the endless, helpless calculation of results which saddens so many a life. If you start with your own canons of procedure, your own criteria of success, your own views of what there is to do, and the notion that you know how it is to be done, depend upon it, God in His love will show you how wrong your forecast was, and, as it seems, destroy your work. You will have to learn the strange and painful lesson that checks and disappointments and failure are part of His plan Who seeks 'not yours, but you,'—not your work, but the surrender of *yourself.* On the other hand, those vices of which you heard this morning, sloth, externalism, vanity, disloyalty to the truth, party spirit, are one and all deprived of the very food on which they live, if, in our work for others, the glory of God in the salvation of souls is the motive power of our lives. Pray that you may realise what Vocation is, not only in the time which yet remains for some of you before you are admitted to the Priesthood, but in and through the whole of your life-work as ministers of God. Remember the ideal of the Christian Priesthood and the secret of the priestly life are hidden in those words of S. Paul, 'I laboured more abundantly than they all ; yet not I, but the grace of God in me.'

# II.

# SERMONS BEFORE
# THE UNIVERSITY OF OXFORD.

# I

# THE VEIL OF MOSES.

'Not as Moses, who put a veil over his face, that the children of Israel could not steadfastly look to the end of that which is abolished. . . . We all, with open face beholding as in a glass the glory of the Lord, are changed into the same image, from glory to glory, even as by the Spirit of the Lord.'—2 COR. iii. 13-18.

OF S. Paul's references to the Old Testament, few are so difficult as his reference to the incident recorded in Exodus xxxiv. According to the Old Testament account, Moses, returning after his sojourn in Mount Sinai, carried with him something of Divine radiance from that Presence in Which he had been. And the people feared to approach him, and were with difficulty persuaded to draw near to hear the message from the Mount. After that, we are told, he 'put a veil on his face,' and only 'when he went in before the Lord' was the veil removed.

Of the moral import of this no hint is given us in the Old Testament, nothing, at least, which could suggest the allegorical interpretation put upon it by S. Paul.

But the fact that an incident of history has been allegorised does not evacuate the allegory of the moral truth it was intended to convey. I proceed to ask,

then, what moral truth, or truths, is S. Paul enforcing
in this allegorical reference to Moses' veil ?

I. S. Paul is comparing the Mosaic and the Christian
revelation ; and he explains the incident thus. The
brightness on the face of Moses was a real, but a
reflected, brightness. It was renewed again and again
when he passed into the Presence of God, and lingered
for a while, as though to mark the Divine authority
with which the revelation of truth was given, and then
vanished away. Yet even this reflected brightness
the Israelites shrank from beholding. They could not
steadfastly behold the face of Moses, and, therefore,
according to S. Paul's interpretation, he yielded to
them, and veiled his face 'so that they could not steadfastly look to the end of that which is abolished.' By
that rejection of God's revelation, that shrinking from
the sight of the truth which God was holding out to
them, they missed the meaning of the whole. First,
they would not, then they could not, see the light
from heaven. Had they dared to 'behold,' they would
have seen the glory fading,—would have realised
not only the truth that Moses came from God, which
in itself was a half-truth, but that the Mosaic dispen-
sation was a preparatory thing, pointing forward to a
glory which should not fade, but increase. And ever
since that day, 'the veil is upon their heart.' They
believe still in the glory of the Mosaic covenant, as if
it were still behind the veil of ceremonies. To them
it is not 'done away,' and therefore the great truth
which lawgiver and prophet again and again proclaimed was lost to them. Their religion became a

superstition. For superstition in religion is nothing but mistaking the means for the end. They did not see that Judaism was stamped with incompleteness; that it pointed forward; that its law of progress was a law of decreasing brightness; that it did not claim to be final. It proclaimed its own transitoriness, its own propædeutic character. It was true only as being a guide to truth; a revelation from God only as throwing the hopes and aspirations of men forward to some fuller truth not yet revealed.

But we, S. Paul argues, speaking as a minister of the Christian revelation, wear no veil. We use great plainness of speech, though 'we reflect as in a mirror' that brighter glory before which the revelation of Moses paled. We, by the reality of our union with Him 'Who is the brightness of God's glory, and the very image of His substance,' appeal to the conscience fearlessly, confidently, 'in the sight of God.' 'For we preach not ourselves, but Christ Jesus as Lord, and ourselves as your servants for Jesus' sake.[1] Seeing it is God, that said, Light shall shine out of darkness, Who shines in our hearts, to give the light of the knowledge of the glory of God in the face of Jesus Christ.'

Comparing, then, the two revelations, S. Paul seems to say that both were real; both were from God; both were bright with the glory of Him Whom they revealed. But they were not equally real, nor equally glorious. The glory of one was an evanescent, fading, transitory thing, a glory which was to be done away;

---

[1] 2 Cor. iv. 5, 6, R.V.

the glory of the other was a permanent, an abiding, an increasing light, changing those on whom it shone from 'glory to glory.' Judaism was either a fragment or a failure; an integral part of the great Christian revelation, or it was nothing. Christianity, on the other hand, claims finality, and yet a finality which is not only consistent with, but implies, a progressive development. To stereotype Christianity with a 'Roma locuta est,' or with a ready 'Act of Uniformity,' is to fetter that which should be a principle of moral and spiritual growth; to make Christianity a phase in the evolution of the human spirit is to despise the birthright of the Christian soul. To change from glory to glory is the ideal of the Christian Church, even as to be conformed to the likeness of Christ is the ideal of the individual Christian.

II. If, now, from S. Paul's allegorising account of the veil of Moses, and his application of it to the Jewish nation, we try to bring out the moral truths which underlie it, we find ourselves naturally and instinctively applying them to our modern days.

1. And, first, he reminds us of the fact that the discovery of a new truth, or the real acceptance of a truth revealed, implies an effort.

In the region of morals we understand at once the need of effort. We know that the freedom of the will, in the only sense in which that often misused term has any meaning, is a freedom to be won by struggle, by moral effort, by resistance to that which fetters and enslaves. Virtue is the successful struggle for self-emancipation; and vice the acquiescence in a life of constantly increasing slavery. But effort is no less

the condition of success in the search for truth. We
are born among the shadows of the Cave, we watch
the shadows pass, we know their order, we have given
them names. Are they not real? We turn to the
light, and we are dazzled. Our sun-filled eyes cannot
bear to look upon it. Take us back to the Cave-world
again, the old familiar world, where we can see. Here
all is strange and new. Our eyes ache with straining.
It cannot be a revelation of truth which implies so
much effort and unrest. ' If God has revealed Himself to man,' it was once said, ' He would have written
His revelation on the sun.' He who uttered those
words meant, I suppose, that a revelation of God must
be simple, and easy to read. But is that ever the
case with truth? And would a revelation written on
the sun be easy for us to read? Could we bear to
look upon it? If we knew that it was there, should
we endure the pain of accustoming our eyes to its
brightness, or should we settle down in contented
ignorance to that which without any effort we can
see? It was this that Israel did. ' Speak thou with
us, but let not God speak.' His Voice is strange and
terrible ; a human voice we are familiar with. Hide
the brightness, the unearthly radiance, which rests
upon the Messenger from God. We can look upon
the veil. They heard the human voice, they looked
upon the veil ; but the voice of God, and the vision of
God, were lost to them.

Effort, moral and intellectual, is the condition of
possessing spiritual truth. There are no doubt
beautiful and holy souls which seem to pass naturally,
and without conscious difficulty, into the vision of

God, changing from glory to glory even in this life, as they reflect the brightness of His presence. But, for most of us, a time of trouble and difficulty and effort comes. We must win our spiritual birthright of truth, even as we must win our moral freedom. In some the moral struggle is the harder,—the effort to be free from passion, pure from defiling sin. In others, who are living pure unselfish lives, the intellectual difficulty fills the whole area of vision ; while in a third class, again, the two kinds of difficulties are strangely interwoven, and each would throw back the responsibility upon the other.

The paramount necessity of a pure heart and good will, for him who is to know the truth, has been sometimes exaggerated till it took the form of what is now derided as ' pectoralism,' or ' pectoral theology.' That ' the pure in heart are blessed, for they shall see God ' ; that ' he who will do God's Will shall know of the doctrine ' ; and, on the other hand, the statement that ' men love darkness rather than light, because their deeds are evil '—these and such like passages are quoted to prove that the moral effort is all that is required. And hence the conclusion was rapidly arrived at, that they who do not accept the full circle of the Christian revelation cannot be living a moral life. Brethren, that Christian charity, for which to-day we pray, and not only Christian charity, but honesty and truth to fact, will not allow that inference to be made. But do not let us forget that in our lives it may be true. No one who has examined himself can have failed to see how, in his own life,

the clearness of his vision of Divine truth has varied
with the variations of his moral character. Charity
forbids us to judge another ; honesty compels us to
judge ourselves. If I cannot see God, if sometimes I
am tempted to ask, Can God be known at all ? is it
not possible that a veil of sin is separating between
my soul and God,—some secret love of evil prejudg-
ing the great issues of that strife which seems to
belong only to the intellectual sphere ? It is not only
in the history of philosophy that Bishop Berkeley's
words hold good : ' First we raise a cloud of dust, and
then we complain we cannot see.' We dare not, then,
and we would not, say that all who reject God's truth
must be guilty of some deep moral sin. We cannot
but believe that they who shrink from the life of
effort, and are content with a low moral level, are
shutting out from themselves the vision of God.

But I am thinking rather of the intellectual than
of the moral effort needed for the rational acceptance
of truth. For it is this which is so often ignored. It
is ignored because, in so many lives, the intellectual
difficulties are not present, and the effort needed for
overcoming them is not felt. On the other hand, as
Bishop Butler says, ' those who are capable, not only
of talking of, but of really seeing, intellectual
difficulties, are capable also of seeing through them.'
And this 'seeing through ' intellectual difficulties needs
an effort as great as that by which we win our moral
freedom. And we are responsible for making it.

Here the conduct of the Israelites, and its consequence, is strangely like what we see going on around

us. They did not mean to reject God's revelation.
Nor do men now openly refuse to make the effort.
They simply let things go. And according to a law
which seems to hold throughout God's world, not to
use a power is to lose it. No one means to destroy
his power of seeing God. Only men do not realise
how much easier it is to weaken than to strengthen
the spiritual sight. We may drift into sin ; we must
strive for holiness. We may drift into ignorance of
God ; we must win our knowledge of Him. 'Invin-
cible ignorance' is generally ignorance which might
once have been overcome.

2. The effort which has to be made is a real one,
and hence men shrink from it. But to refuse to make
the effort is to lose the vision of the truth. This is
S. Paul's second principle. The knowledge of God,
revealed in Christ, comes to us with a claim to
authority. It wears a supernatural glory on its face,
and our eyes shrink from the sight. It is not like
the truth that we know. All other truths we may
question and challenge. We may interrogate the
witnesses, and call upon them to prove their point.
But revealed truth calls for submission, seems to
check at the outset that spirit of free inquiry which
we pursue elsewhere. As reasonable men, then, we
hesitate. We cannot abandon our right of private
judgment. Be it so. But what follows ? If to examine into that which professes to be Divine truth
is a right which every man may claim, it is also a duty
for which every man is responsible. The assertion
of an inalienable right of private judgment is the

admission of an inalienable duty of spiritual effort. And what do we see? Just at the moment when men, rightly or wrongly, are least ready to take great spiritual truths on trust, there is also less readiness to search earnestly for spiritual truth for ourselves. The division of labour which has become necessary in knowledge has familiarised men's minds with the idea of marking off some parts or parcels of knowledge with which they have nothing to do. And by a false analogy the knowledge of God is treated as one of these parcels, as though it belonged to theologians, not to ordinary men. Yet the vision of God is for all. It is not a special science, nor a prize to be run for by privileged competitors, nor a gift that is given to a favoured few. It is that for which man lives, in which he finds his only good. The only rational correlative, then, to the rejection of an authority we believe to be false is the willingness to spare no effort in the search for what is true.

Such a willingness there was in the great revolt against traditionalism, with which modern science is said to have begun. Those who rejected the scholastic teaching about Nature were ready to throw themselves eagerly and hopefully into the search for truth. Self-discipline, moral and intellectual, earnest, persistent experimentation, a great reverence for Nature, whose servant and interpreter man claimed to be, the abandoning of all short and easy methods, the sure belief that Nature could be known—these were the principles of the new science which was to replace the old. And it has won the triumphs it deserved.

E

So it was for a time even in the matter of religious truth. The real reformer not only abandoned what he believed to be false, he devoted himself honestly and faithfully to a new search for the true. He believed that God had revealed Himself to man, and he set forward with resolute unshrinking effort to recover that truth, by the reverent study of the Word of God, and the teaching of the primitive Church.

It is different now. Men claim still the right to criticise and to destroy; they think lightly of the responsibility which that involves. They do not care to face the difficulty, and so they shut their eyes, or look another way. Or else self-confidence takes the place of self-devotion: self-confidence, that most fatal barrier to the knowledge of the truth. We see it around us every day. The airy rejection of all that saints wrought out by prayer and fasting and communion with God, is consistent with a tone and temper which, in any other department of life, would be the mark of shallowness and self-satisfied ignorance. One man, with the Bible under his arm, sets out cheerfully to recast the Creeds of Christendom. Another finds that he can do the same without burdening himself with a book. 'O Luther, great art thou,' cries one; 'thou hast delivered us from the bondage to a Church, who will deliver us from the bondage to a book?' For those who ask that question, the answer is not far to seek. We can mark the different 'moments' in the evolution of self-will. There is an *evangelical* moment, when the Bible, uncritically accepted, is appealed to against the faith of

Christendom, and the *critical* moment, when the Bible is rejected bit by bit, because it will not square with some preconceived idea ; and the *dogmatic* moment, when the individual seats himself on the throne of infallibility, with the confident *L'Eglise, c'est moi.*

That is, of course, an extreme case. The mass of those who start with the rejection of traditional Christianity will not go so far as this. There are less defiant, if not less fatal, ways by which men avoid the duty of the search for God. For instance, a large number of men shrink with true humility from all that looks like self-assertion. If they cannot accept the faith of the Church, at least they will not set up a faith of their own. They will not explain away supernaturalism, or deny the existence of spiritual truth. But neither will they be so 'uncharitable' as to take sides in such a difficult matter. And so, out of mere charity and self-distrust, they take refuge in vagueness. They will be undogmatic and unsectarian, their religion, 'a nimbus of golden mist,' not bright enough to dazzle the eye ; their theology with no definite lines which might intersect the lines of philosophy, or science, or ordinary practice. And soon they cannot understand why people should trouble themselves with theological problems, when there is such an easy way out of it all. Yes! it is easy, and the knowledge of truth requires effort. It is easy to be 'an honorary member of all creeds,' just as it is easy to be a sleeping partner in a firm of eminent religious respectability. It is easy to think of questions as infinitesimally little, when we know infinitesimally little about them ; it is easier than to profess a definite creed which would at least require a minimum of external conformity.

On the other hand, it is so hard to be honest with ourselves ; to force ourselves to look stedfastly at some spiritual truth which, if established, will re-cast, perhaps, practice and theory alike ; to compel ourselves to be definite in what we do believe, be it much or little, and, instead of cataloguing the dogmas we have renounced, to realise that spiritual truth we still retain ; to look it full in the face, and allow it to be reflected in our life. Again and again men have recovered their faith, and have by God's grace been brought back to the full knowledge of Him, because they made the effort to be true to their own light. But life, with all its crowding interests, is not long enough for this. There is so much to tax our energies. We cannot spend so much effort on religion. And so the power to see truth is weakened by disuse, and, at last, we settle down to the belief that spiritual truth is the only sphere in which a premium is set upon what is hazy and obscure. Precision in science, exact thought in philosophy, minute accuracy in scholarship, a jealous care for the details of historical fact, plain straightforward truthfulness in the Law Courts, firmness and decision in the ordinary acts of life, absolute indefiniteness in religion, and a theology of platitudes,—that is what our age admires.

And when we have come thus to put vagueness in place of definiteness, we have our reward. We are

not troubled like other men. We are on excellent
terms with philosophy and science, and criticism and
history. Palæontology does not conflict with our
view of Genesis. Historical criticism is nothing to
us. Metaphysics cannot touch our faith. A religion
which has come to be something between a poem and
a picture-gallery is safe from ordinary attacks.

But the very process which has made it safe from
attack makes it also of little worth as a moral power.
The storage of spiritual force is somehow strangely
connected with a definite faith. And a religion which
offers no points of attack is a religion which offers
little power of resistance. Hence the shrinking from
that effort which is necessary for making our faith
definite too often ends in a willingness to explain it
away. Is such a luminous haze worth having? If
all our knowledge is definite knowledge, what can be
the value to a reasonable man of a faith which refuses
to be defined? And so men pass into the dogmatic
rejection of Divine truth. Loss of heat does not
make that impalpable haze condense into a solar
system. But the haze tends to disappear. It is
always easy to explain away what is different from
the life in which we live, and especially easy when it
has little practical bearing on that life. A positivism
which denies everything which it cannot touch, and
taste, and handle; a natural science of man which
ignores all that is distinctive of humanity; a theory
of morals which puts aside the supernatural forces
which have made morality what it is—these are but
samples of the way in which men avoid intellectual

effort. They are short cuts to infallibility, as John
Locke would call them, and they win for us that
which Bacon sneers at as 'the satisfaction which men
call truth.' But the real result is the paralysis of
those powers of our rational life in which our greatness lies. We indolently shrink from effort, and try
to justify our sloth.

There is not one of the 'Idola' of the individual or
of the race which will not help to hinder us from
knowing God. The desire for a symmetrical theory
of the world, the readiness to prove a wished-for conclusion true, the unwillingness to test and try, the
restlessness of superficial theorising, or the predominant influence of some special study—all these beset
us in our search for God. Yet the self-discipline
which has been the condition of progress in science
and philosophy is to be dispensed with in that which
alone concerns us all—the knowledge of God. Surely
if it is our duty to clear the mind of all that would
hinder us from a serious study of nature, it is not less
a duty to do the same before we draw near to the
presence of God.

III. Finally, if the knowledge of God implies an
effort, and if the abandoning that effort, or the belief
that it is useless, is to lose the vision of the truth, two
consequences seem to follow :—

(*a*) If I appeal to authority, I must appeal to those
whose lives have been devoted to the search for the
vision of God. Fearlessly and in His sight I claim
my right of private judgment to estimate the relative
value of those who seek to guide me in religious

things. I know that in the last resort all truth is one, but I see that there are two departments in which men seek for truth, and, till the unity of both is reached, I will not sacrifice one part to conform it to another. We have learned much from experience. If the scholastic age has taught us not to go to theology for our science, the present age is clearly teaching us not to go to science for our theology. It would be surely as much a mark of intellectual feebleness and relaxation of moral fibre, to accept the *obiter dicta* of a scientific teacher as authoritative in matters of religious truth, as to give a Divine authority to the details of the Mosaic cosmogony. I will not go to Moses or to David, to S. Paul or to S. John, to S. Augustine or to S. Thomas, on a question of embryology, or palæontology, or the origin of species. Neither will I go to the priests of the science of nature to solve me the perplexities of my moral and spiritual life. ' Man is a part of nature, but he is more.' Theology as a branch of anthropology may serve as a convenient theme for an article in a Review; the development of religion out of the worship of an ancestral ghost may be worthy occupation for the leisure hours of a great biologist. But the needs of the soul are not met, but mocked, by such a *tour de force*. Sooner would I believe that the world of visible things in which I live is a phantasmagoria, and science with its great discoveries a splendid poem, than explain away those spiritual realities which are

' Closer to me than breathing, nearer than hands and feet.'

The consciousness of sin, the longing for God, the deep moral questionings of the human spirit, will not yield to arguments like these. They have not the unvarying note of truth. They do not give power; they confess impotence. The divining-rod with which those great leaders smote the rock of nature, and set loose its hidden springs, in the region of moral and spiritual truth, seems to have lost its cunning. The strong arm which could lift the gates of Gaza becomes weak as that of a woman or a child. They have shown us, those priests of science, nobly and well, the glories of nature, 'the living garment of God,' but when we ask them to show us His face, they put us off with a discussion of the texture of the veil.

We turn from them in disappointment to those, men sometimes of less intellectual calibre, certainly men who knew less about the science of nature, and who yet with a strange power have touched the springs of human life, and opened up its unknown depths of self-sacrifice and love ; men who, in all the beauty of a supernatural radiance, seem, as we look upon them, to change from glory to glory. These are they who, in a long line, have declared to us the truth of God as they had seen it. They did not shrink, in weakness or in doubt, from the effort of beholding the glory of the Lord in the face of Jesus Christ. ' There is no proof,' it has been said, 'that a thing is visible, but that men have seen it.' There is no proof that God is knowable, save that men have known Him.

(*b*) And yet that proof is no proof till we ourselves

have seen and known. As against those who would resolve religion into illusion, and deny the possibility of seeing God, we may indeed appeal to lives lived in the sunlight of His countenance, and reflecting, with unveiled face, the brightness of His glory. And yet the saints who lived with God, nay, even He Himself Who came from the bosom of the Father, can only declare the truth. No power on earth, or in heaven, can compel us to see God, or save us from the effort of beholding Him for ourselves. The Church may indeed preserve and hand on the deposit of the truth which Jesus Christ revealed ; only our own effort can make that truth our own. And here we may claim upon our side the most universally admitted fact of morals. Conformity to a moral law, however pure and noble, is not morality; obedience to the authority of a Church, however true, is not religion. A creed unrealised is a truth unknown. That is the great fact which they have seized who reject authority. For some men reject truth in their earnest striving after it. They put aside the Christian Creeds because for them a truth external is no truth at all. And surely in this, at least, they are right. Yet, thank God, if many who profess the Church's Creed know less of God than they profess, there are many who reject the Creed who know far more than they are willing to allow.

With them, and with every earnest soul which yearns for the vision of God, we may agree in this. Not in submission to external truth, not in obedience to the Church's faith, not in the imitation of the

holiest saints, does the vision of God consist. These
are but the means by which He would make visible
His truth, and break down the barrier of self-will,
that we may see Him for ourselves. Only when, with
unveiled face, we reflect, as in a mirror, the glory of the
Lord, are we changed into the same image from glory
to glory, and at last are made like Him when we see
Him as He is.

## II.

# THE GOD OF PHILOSOPHY

AND

# THE GOD OF RELIGION.

' He that cometh to God must believe that He is, and that He is a
rewarder of them that diligently seek Him.'—Heb. xi. 6.

THE knowledge of God, which constitutes religion,
implies, as the condition of its growth, moral and
intellectual effort: moral effort, because 'the pure in
heart' alone can 'see God'; intellectual effort, that the
knowledge of Him may be a true and integral part
of our rational possession. If the separation of faith
and life is the sure forerunner of moral dissolution,
the separation of faith from reason is the destruction
of real religion. And they who in our day would
make for us a division of territory between what we
know and what we believe, and bid us keep our
religion distinct from our philosophy and our science,
might as well suggest that we should adopt what
creed we please, but be very careful that it does not
in any way affect our conduct. For a thinking man
who believes in religion either separation is impossible. Faith is not faith if it does not characterise
life; while a belief which stands outside reason is all
one with that which is irrational. The unknowable,

whether we judge it by practical or speculative tests, is the non-existent ; and religion stands or falls with the possibility of a real knowledge of God.

But to claim for religion a real knowledge of God, as distinct from that faith which some oppose to knowledge, lays us open at once to two serious objections.

I. First, it may be said, religion on its own confession rests not on reason, but on faith, and the Church rejects as Gnosticism or rationalism the claim of reason to dispense with faith. The Bible, from end to end, is full of the record of those who triumphed by faith, from Abraham, the father of the faithful, to those who, ' having not seen, yet believed ' in the risen Christ. They were men who ' walked by faith, and not by sight,' and their faith not only overcame the world, but seemed to glory in setting at naught the evidence before them. This mysterious faith is, moreover, spoken of as ' the gift of God,' without which ' it is impossible to please Him.' Faith thus becomes the very groundwork on which religion rests. It is the very presupposition of the knowledge of God, since ' he that cometh to God must believe that He is, and that He is a rewarder of them that diligently seek Him.' Here we are dealing not with the deductions of theology, or the coherence of a religious system, but with that without which neither theology nor religion has any existence—the knowledge of God. And we are to start, in plain words, by begging the question, making, at the outset, an assumption which we cannot prove, that God is, and that He is a Being Who stands in a certain definite relation with man.

It would seem as if, supposing this to be true, religion is bound in honesty to abandon its claim to knowledge, and retire into the fastness of faith. For in all our rational processes our boast is that we will have no foregone conclusions, that we start without prepossessions, that we are anxious only to be guided by the evidence, that we have exchanged the school-man's *crede ut intelligas* for that modern counsel of perfection, 'Doubt everything till you have proved it.'

It is so rarely that men concern themselves with the presuppositions of familiar processes, that this contrast between the method of faith and the method of reason seems to many to imply a fundamental opposition between the two. Yet we have only to look a little below the surface to see that the contrast is superficial and unreal. There is no need in this place to speak of that which, if we are to believe those who have written on the logic of empirical science, is 'the ultimate major premiss of all inductions,' and which is itself an assumption justified only by the fruitfulness of its results, an assumption, more-over, which only fits the facts when under the term 'uniform' we include its contradictory, the 'infinitely various.' For the truth is that the so-called Law of Uniformity is not the fundamental assumption of the rational interpretation of nature, nor of any rational process whatsoever.

But there is a fundamental assumption which

underlies not only that which, by an abuse of terms, we commonly call *science*, but all reasoning which is not abstract but real, the assumption, namely, that the environment in which we live is a rational and intelligible whole, something which our reason may hope to interpret more and more perfectly. That initial act of faith, for it is nothing less, is the pre-supposition of all our reasoning. He who comes to the study of nature must believe in the rational unity of that which he would rationally explain. Without that belief reason is helpless. And the same pre-supposition is more consciously present to the philosopher, when, in spite of apparent contradictions, and in face of the existence of a dualism which to the ordinary man is without history and without hope, he presses forward in the belief that there is a real and rational unity in all that is. To accept a dualism as ultimate is for him the paralysis of reason, as complete as for a scientific man to believe that nature is the work of chance, or the complex result of the incalculable vagaries of unknowable, because irrational, spirits.

It is the unswerving belief in that first assumption, the fearless acting upon that initial act of faith, which makes possible the progress of science and philosophy. Reason cannot doubt the possibility of rationalising without an act of intellectual suicide.

When men ask, 'Is God knowable?' they are dis-appointed and surprised at being told that 'God can-not be discovered by a process ending with Q. E. D.'; and they look upon it as a sign of weakness in the

evidences of religion. But if we turn round upon
them with the question, Is knowledge possible? or,
Is Nature knowable? they are content to point to the
fact of knowledge. We *can* interpret the world in
which we live. We have found out some of Nature's
secrets ; we believe that we shall find out more. The
'region of nescience' is daily contracting its borders.
If our knowledge is as yet imperfect, it is not because
Nature cannot be known, but because we have not yet
found the clue. We press forward with unabated
hope. It is futile to ask, Is knowledge possible?
Hume's answer to the Pyrrhonist is sufficient for
such childish and captious quibbling. 'These
principles may flourish and triumph in the schools,
where it is, indeed, difficult, if not impossible, to
refute them ; but as soon as they leave the shade,
and by the presence of the real objects, which actuate
our passions and sentiments, are put in opposition to
the more powerful principles of our nature, they
vanish like smoke, and leave the most determined
sceptic in the same condition as other mortals.' [1]

We may say the same for the knowledge of God.
The question, Is God knowable? is, no doubt a fruitful subject for discussion in 'the schools.' Treated *a
priori*, it is like the airy discussion of the possibility
of knowledge by those who calmly and contentedly
ignore all that science is doing, and has done. But they
who are content to justify their presupposition by the
fruitfulness of its result, cannot call religion irrational
if it is unable to demonstrate the truth in which it rests.

[1] *Concerning Human Understanding*, § 12.

Our first difficulty, then, that religion claims to rest on faith, while science and philosophy rest on reason, may fairly be answered thus. The 'faith' of the Bible is not the irrational thing which some would make it, else it would not claim to be the correlative of truth. And, if the claim of a rational process to be true is not inconsistent with the undemonstrated belief in the reality of its object and the trustworthiness of reason, the validity of religion is no less consistent with the undemonstrated belief that 'God is, and that He is a rewarder of them that diligently seek Him.' Religion does not ask whether God is, or whether He is knowable—questions, indeed, which are not two, but one. It is concerned with the questions how God is revealed to man, what they have declared to us about Him who have known Him best, how much they have to tell us who have most truly followed the natural light of conscience, what we may learn from those whose conscience had been quickened and informed by the revelation of the Old Testament or from that full unfolding of God's nature by Him, the Light of the World, Who came from the bosom of the Father to declare His love. Religion has no answer to one who says, 'First prove to me that God exists, before you ask me to try and know Him.'

II. But in advancing the claim of rationality for religion, we are met by a second and more serious difficulty. Philosophy claims, as religion does, a knowledge of God. Even science, as it outgrows the swaddling-clothes of positivism, and becomes metaphysical, tends to do the same. It requires no special knowledge of science to enable an onlooker to see that the old atomistic and mechanical theories of nature which satisfied our fathers will not fit the biological categories under which men now think of nature. Hence there is considerable anxiety evinced by certain people to discover a middle term by which to pass from materialist premises to something like an idealist conclusion. Christian theology, which neither grants the premises nor identifies itself with the conclusion, can afford to look on and watch these efforts. And the main result is a movement of science in the direction of the once hated metaphysics, and the recognition by both of a rational unity in the world, to which, save for the religious associations of the word, we might give the name of God. But the God of philosophy is not the God of religion ; and the God which conscience demands is not at once identifiable with that which science and philosophy alike tend to recognise. Hence religion mistrusts philosophy. If here and there a S. Paul, or a S. Clement of Alexandria, or a S. Athanasius, or a S. Basil dares to claim philosophy for Christ, there are numbers whose profound distrust of reason would express itself in Tertullian's saying, ' *Hæreti- corum patriarchæ philosophi*,'[1] or would take refuge in the perhaps unconscious deism of Bacon, when he advises us to render to reason what belongs to reason, and to faith what belongs to faith, ' lest from the unwholesome blending of things human and divine

---

[1] *Adv. Hermogenem*, cap. 8.

F

there result not only a phantastical philosophy, but an heretical religion.'[1] In the present day there are not wanting those who would recommend a similar division of territory. It is the easiest and most indolent, and at the same time most suicidal, way of evading an intellectual difficulty. It is to talk as if the wounds of reason could be salved by an irrational faith, and a God whom we cannot know might yet somehow be the object of belief.

Such a severance between two parts of our nature, whether suggested by the friends or foes of religion, is impossible for many. And it is terrible where it is possible. It is the state described as his own by Jacobi, in a well-known passage. 'There is light in my heart,' he says, 'but when I seek to bring it into the understanding it is extinguished. Which illumination is the true one—that of the understanding, which discloses well-defined and fixed shapes, but behind them an abyss; or that of the heart, which, while it sends forth rays of promise upwards, is unable to supply the want of definite knowledge?' 'Which illumination is the true one?' That is the torturing question which will recur again and again to those who have thus set their conscience against their reason. It is impossible to be 'a heathen with the understanding, but a Christian with the spirit.' Such a state of *unstable* equilibrium cannot be maintained. To modern ears it sounds almost like the despair of reason when the great author of the *Apologia* confesses, 'Were it not for the voice speaking

[1] *De Augmentis Scientiarum*, iii. 2.

so clearly in my conscience and my heart, I should be an atheist, or a pantheist, or a polytheist, when I looked upon the world.'[1]

It cannot be that man has to choose between a faith which overrides reason and a reason which destroys faith. Yet the contrast between the God of religion and conscience and the God of philosophy and reason is a real one, and it is worth while to examine more closely wherein the contrast consists.

The conception of God which underlies religion is first and before all that of a Being Who is, at least, so far like ourselves that He can hear us when we speak to Him, can understand our wants, and our sorrows, and our struggles. The God Whom our conscience seeks to know is before all things a *moral* Being. Nor is it any contradiction to this fact that there are found peoples who do not recognise the unity of God, or that there are primitive religions which travesty His nature, or conceive of it anthropomorphically even after they have attained to the truth that God is One. And the Old Testament view of God, which, because it is so much higher and purer than man's natural conception of Him, we speak of as a revelation, confirms the highest truth to which the conscience had attained as to the unity of God. Slowly, but surely, it strips off all which conscience tells us is unworthy of a true humanity, while it maintains and expands the belief in the personal relation of God with man. If this is anthropomorphism Religion must bear the charge. God is still revealed as 'a God that heareth

---

[1] Newman, *Apologia*, Part vii.

prayer'; as One Who does not think it beneath Him
to watch over and to guide the education of the
human race; as the All-Father of humanity, not in
the vague generalised sense in which He may be
called the Father of all creation, but as standing in
a unique relation to us His children, which already
implies something of a common nature between us
and Him.   When a great heretic compared the
relation of God to man with that which man bears to
the *scarabæus*, he fancied he was exalting the majesty
of God, though in truth he was cutting away the
roots of morality and religion.   The Bible pictures to
us the relation of God to man as being from first to
last a moral relation.   It never raises the question
whether moral attributes can be applied to God.   It
assumes His moral nature as it assumes His personal
being.   Nature with its ordered sequence of cause
and effect, laws without which natural science is
impossible, the uniformity, the coherence, the intel-
ligibility of nature as an organised whole—everything
is subordinated to the one dominant thought of the
omnipresence of God, and His care for the creatures
He has made in His likeness.   Familiarised as we
are with the language of modern science, trained
to expect unity and order and law everywhere, it
seems strange to turn to the Bible and find every
fact in nature ascribed immediately to the will of
God.   Those observed uniformities which we, in our
realistic way, have come to think of as somehow
controlling nature, are elastic and pliant under His
hand.   The moral purpose is everywhere supreme

over physical order, not merely as if it were a higher
power to which the physical is compelled to yield
unwilling submission, but as that in which the
physical order finds its own *raison d'être.* The
miracles which gather round the great epochs in the
history of Israel are in perfect keeping with the view
which runs through the Nature-psalms. And when
the purpose of God reaches its climax in the Life and
Death and Resurrection of Jesus Christ, even that
which to us is the miracle of miracles, the miracle of
Easter Day, is spoken of by S. Peter, not as a great
exception, but as a thing which could not but have
happened, since it was not possible that He Who was
the Resurrection and the Life should be holden by the
chains of death. To that moral view of nature, that
which seems to us most difficult is most natural ; for
the Deism which has dominated thought in England
for two centuries and a half has accustomed us to
think of nature, not as the manifestation of a God Who
is everywhere present in it, but as a huge complex of
interacting forces, or a curiously complicated piece of
mechanism which has somehow broken away from
the Maker of the machine.

If, now, from what we may call the moral and
religious conception of the world, we turn to that
which is more distinctly philosophical, and ask, What
does our intellectual, in abstraction from our moral,
nature postulate in God ? we answer at once *rational
unity and coherence.* Whether we adopt the language
of a materialism which is unconsciously giving way
to pantheism, and speak of God as 'The Ultimate

Reality,' or 'The Infinite and Eternal Energy,' or
'The Inscrutable Existence everywhere manifested';
or whether, in the language of a far different philosophy, we speak of the Absolute Idea or the Eternal
Consciousness, that which our thought dwells upon is
the thought of God as the Unity of Nature.  But we
shrink from ascribing to Him those attributes in
which the religious consciousness takes delight ; philosophy fears the anthropomorphism implied in the
thought of God as a Person to Whom we can apply
such terms as just, and holy, and wise, and loving, a
God of tender mercies, a Father of compassion.  If
we use the terms still, they are divested of half their
meaning.  Even personality must be explained to
mean something which is indistinguishable from its
opposite.  For 'personality,' we are told, implies
limitation, and an infinite personality is a contradiction in terms.

This contrast between the God Whom religion
craves for, and the God Whom philosophy demands,
is fraught with serious consequences.  Many of you
will bear me out when I say that those who in youth
and early manhood have learned to think of God as
Christians think of Him, who have been used to go
to Him as 'a God that heareth prayer,' are puzzled
and distressed, when they begin to read philosophy,
to find how little room there is, in the philosophical
conception of God, for that thought of Him which
had been the basis of their religion, and the starting-
point of their spiritual life.  And they find themselves compelled to re-construct their theology, with
the result, too often, that after a few terms spent in

learning the alphabet of philosophy, the definite religious conception of God is put aside, or fades away into something vague and meaningless, disguised under an unrealised philosophical name.

And surely the insufficiency of our own teaching is largely to blame for this. Sons are lost to the Church of Christ, not because they will not have her teaching, but because they do not know what her teaching is. To our age Pantheism is infinitely more attractive, because more rational and more human, than the Deism of a past generation. And probably the vast majority of those who reject Christianity on philosophical grounds do so because, as popularly taught, it seems to deny what is true in Pantheism, and to be itself almost identified with Deism. Yet the truth is exactly the reverse. The God of religion and revelation, the God revealed in Holy Scripture and the teaching of the Catholic Church, has nothing in common with that deistic conception against which philosophy protests. God is everywhere present in the world which He has made—' In Him we live, and move, and have our being.' He is the Life of our life, the rational unity of the world, the secret force of all creation. He is all that our intellectual nature seeks for in its desire to explain, to render intelligible, the world around us. And yet He is all that conscience demands, a Being with moral attributes, Who can be the object of faith and hope and love. Christianity fearlessly holds both sides of the contradiction, if it be a contradiction, that God is everywhere present in the world, and yet is not identical with it. 'God the Word,' says S. Athanasius, 'so far from being contained by anything, contains all things Himself. He is in the whole of creation, since, though distinct in being from the universe, He is yet present in all things by His power; giving order to all things, and over all, and in all, revealing His own providence; giving life at once to each and all, including the whole without being included, but being wholly and completely in His Father alone.'[1]

God, as the Truth of the universe, is the object of science and philosophy, no less than of religion. Pantheism itself cannot go beyond the Christian teaching as to God's omnipresence in nature by the Logos. But the conscience demands more than Pantheism can give; nay, it demands that which Pantheism, by identifying God with the universe, is compelled to deny. 'My soul is athirst for God, for the Living God,' not a First Cause or an *Etre Suprême*, outside and away from our troubled human life, not even an immanent spiritual unity such as satisfies my intellectual craving for a rational explanation of the world, but a Living God, a Heart which can answer to the beating of my heart, a supreme object of love, Who is Himself love; a personal God in Whom I can trust as I can trust no earthly friend; One Who will be ever near me in life; to Whom in the hour of death I may commend my spirit; One Whom, among all the changes and chances of this mortal life, I may know as a God of love Who changeth not.

'I will not argue with that man,' said John Locke,

---

[1] *De Incarnatione*, cap. xvii.

'who refuses to accept a truth because he cannot reconcile it with some other truth.' And yet the imperious demand of our whole rational nature to see all truth as one cannot be set aside. Whatever may have been possible in former days, we cannot accept two truths, any more than we can believe in two Gods. We must, then, bring that demand of conscience which underlies religion into organic relation with that which we call reason. And that, as it seems to me, can only be when we accustom ourselves to see in conscience and reason, not typical opposites, as some would tell us, but different workings of our whole self-conscious rational nature. We may not indeed confuse the spheres. It is no longer possible, by a rough-and-ready argument from Design, to find the moral character and personality of God in the rational coherence of external nature. And we are slowly learning the converse truth, that it is futile to seek to find the discoveries of modern science embedded in the precious teaching of Holy Scripture. But neither is thereby rendered false or unnecessary.

Yet it is impossible for a Christian teacher to shut his eyes to the fact that the real danger of our day, a danger intensified by the speculative activity around us, is the atrophy of conscience. While our intellectual powers are being trained and exercised in every possible way, the moral reason is more and more being left to take care of itself. Bishop Butler and Kant, more than any philosophical teachers since S. Thomas Aquinas, have vindicated the claim of

conscience to be a rational power, worthy to be
trusted in its own domain. And yet in spite of this
the case for conscience too often goes by default.
First, we allow ourselves to think of it as a lower
function of reason, if not itself irrational, and then we
cease to believe that it is an organ of truth at all.

My brothers, it is your work, it is our work as
Christian men, against the μονοκωλία of mere intel-
lectualism, to vindicate the truth of conscience, and
to prove it in our lives. As Christians we believe that
to rest in simple trust upon the Father's love, to
know Him as a God of never-failing mercies and
unchanging goodness, is a broader, deeper, fuller
truth than any to which the speculative reason can
attain. The religious view of God not only does not
contradict, it contains, it justifies, but it also *extends*
that view which, for many, is all that they can know
of God. While we think of Him only as the omni-
present Power of all that is, we may bow before Him
in wondering awe, and perhaps mistake that awe for
worship. We may speak of Him in language borrowed from the religious fervour of the saints, as
before now speculation has pirated the terms of Christian theology ; but we cannot love Him, for love is a
personal thing ; we cannot go to Him as to a Friend
when the world looks dark and cheerless, or stay
ourselves on Him when all else that we have known
is fading from our sight. It is easier to make religion
philosophical than to make philosophy in any real
sense religious.

It is our work, my brothers, to show that the life of

faith is also in the fullest sense a rational life ; a life which carries with it and in it those great principles of reason, without which science and philosophy would cease to be. And more than this God calls on us to do. He calls upon us to prove His existence to the world in the only way in which it can be proved. For as every truth we wrest from nature, every triumph which reason wins, is a new witness to the truth with which reason starts, so every life lived in the light of God's presence, every self-sacrificing effort made in the power of God's love, every holy character which 'reflects as in a mirror' the character of God, is a new assurance that 'He is, and that He is a rewarder of them that diligently seek Him.'

# III

## THE CLAIM TO AUTHORITY.

'And they come again to Jerusalem: and as He was walking in the Temple, there come to Him the chief priests, and the scribes, and the elders, and say unto Him, By what authority doest Thou these things? and who gave Thee this authority to do these things? And Jesus answered and said unto them, I will also ask of you one question, and answer Me, and I will tell you by what authority I do these things. The baptism of John, was it from Heaven, or of men? answer Me.'—S. MARK xi. 27-30.

THE teaching of Jesus Christ differed from that of His contemporaries in a remarkable way. He had no position, if we may use such a word of Him Who was the Truth of God : He was neither scribe nor Pharisee, yet He criticised both, He censured both, and in His own teaching, as even ordinary hearers felt, 'He taught them as one having authority, and not as the scribes.' He was no mere exponent of Moses. When He interpreted the Law it was as one who spoke from a higher platform. In the presence of Christ the Son Moses was but as a servant. And the Son alone can fully explain the servant's message. He can, as it were, pass beyond the fact to the reason of the fact. Moses permitted divorce, but divorce was not in the eternal law of God, though Moses,

because of the hardness of men's hearts, suffered men
to put away their wives. But Christ does more than
explain why the Mosaic Law was what it was. He
corrects and supplements it, claiming in the Sermon
on the Mount to set Himself on the level of Him
from Whom Moses came. 'It was said to them of
old time, but I say unto you.' And as Christ refused
to shelter Himself behind Moses, so neither would
He claim His authority from the father of the faithful. Both in time and in authority He was before
Abraham. Which was the greater paradox? 'Your
father Abraham ·rejoiced to see My day, and he saw
it, and was glad.' Certainly a Teacher Who could
declare that Abraham looked for Him and Moses
spoke of Him claimed an authority of which scribe
and Pharisee never dreamed.

And Christ's acts, no less than His words, implied
the same. Is not the Sabbath of Divine appointment,
older even than the Mosaic law? Yet Christ, in the
judgment of the accredited guardians of the Law,
breaks the Sabbath, not only for acts of mercy, and
justifies Himself in it, since 'the Son of Man is Lord
also of the Sabbath.' He dares to do even that
which is God's sole prerogative. For 'who can forgive sins but God only?' Yet Christ says with
authority, 'Thy sins are forgiven thee.' Either, as
the Pharisees said, it is blasphemy, or He rightly
claimed a Divine authority—inherent, not derived.

This challenge, then, 'By what authority?' 'Who
gave Thee this authority?' seems to mark the final
attempt of the chief priests, the scribes, and the

elders to discredit the great Teacher in the eyes of
the people. Truth speaks to men in its own majesty,
its own authority, its own right. To challenge that
authority is already to have prejudged its claim.
Neither truth nor goodness can support their claim
by what is commonly called proof. To question their
authority is to have passed beyond their range. This
the opponents of Christ had done. The triumphal
entry was over. The trodden palm branches were
yet unwithered. The Hosannas seemed yet ringing
in the people's ears, when the representatives of the
Jewish hierarchy gathered themselves together and
openly before the people challenged the claims of
Christ. ' By what authority doest Thou these things ?
and who gave Thee this authority ?'

It was the climax of opposition between the new
and the old, the Judaism which was passing away
and the Kingdom of Christ which was to take its
place. In spirit at least it was far removed from
such questions as from time to time had been heard
from the lips of doubting disciples. In the early
days of Christ's preaching even His great forerunner
John Baptist had sent to Him with the question,
' Art Thou He that should come, or do we look for
another ?' More than once too His own disciples,
half-doubting, half-believing, had asked for some
final resolution of their doubt : ' If Thou be the Christ,
tell us plainly.' And the people again and again
had asked for a sign in corroboration of Christ's
mission. But in all these there was, if not faith, at
least the willingness to be convinced, and therefore

they stand in sharp contrast with the challenge of the scribes and Pharisees, ' By what authority ? '

Once indeed, in our Lord's earthly life, had a like challenge been uttered, like in spirit if not in words. It was at the opening of His ministry, when the anti-Christian forces of the world were ideally summed up in its Prince, that in the dark mysterious conflict of the wilderness the utter antagonism between light and darkness might be revealed ; when the Personal Power of evil gathered his forces against the Christ of God, and challenged Him to prove His Godhead : ' If Thou be the Son of God, turn stones into bread.' ' Cast Thyself down.'

Once again, at the close of Christ's public life, the same spirit reappears. It is no longer now a challenge, but a taunt. Unbelief has given way to triumphant malice. He Who claimed to be the Son of God is dying the malefactor's death. It is the moment of the world's triumph, and it uses its advantage : ' If Thou be the Son of God, come down from the cross.' 'He saved others, let Him save Himself if He be Christ, the chosen of God.'

The challenge of the scribes and Pharisees is one in spirit with that of the Tempter, and with the taunts of the crucifiers. Yet Christ treats it differently. The Tempter He rebukes with the thrice-repeated ' It is written.' Before the crucifiers He is silent, and answers nothing. But with the Pharisees and scribes He consents to argue—not indeed for their sake, but for the sake of those who heard the question. A public challenge calls for a public answer, and Christ meets it by a question: 'I will also ask of you one question, and answer Me, and I will tell you by what authority I do these things. The baptism of John, was it from Heaven, or of men? answer Me.'

The dilemma was obvious. To confess the supernatural character of John Baptist's teaching was not only to admit the principle of authority, but was also to admit by implication the claims of Him Whose advent John declared; while to deny its supernatural character was to bring themselves into direct collision with the newly aroused Messianic hopes of the people. That the scribes and elders themselves rejected the prophetic claim of the Baptist the Evangelist clearly implies. But prudential reasons compelled them to conceal their scepticism. 'They feared the people, for all men counted John that he was a prophet indeed. And they answered and said unto Jesus, We cannot tell.' It is easier to take refuge in agnosticism than to face the consequences of either of the two contradictory alternatives. The scribes and Pharisees had not the courage of their opinions. They answered, 'We cannot tell. And Jesus, answering, saith unto them, Neither do I tell you by what authority I do these things.'

In our day the question is heard again. For the religion of Jesus Christ claims, as He claimed, to speak with authority. It challenges submission; it lays claim to absolute truth; it has the courage to say that it rests not on sensible experience; that its facts are eternally true, though they can neither be examined under the microscope nor weighed in the

scales, nor subjected to spectrum analysis, nor laid
bare by the scalpel of the biologist. In the consciousness of its Divine authority it presumes to reverse
the common ratio of value between the here and the
hereafter, teaching that 'the things which are seen
are temporal, but the things which are not seen are
eternal.' Moreover, the body in which the eternal
truth abides claims to be a Divine Society, indwelt
by the Spirit of Christ, its ministers stewards of
God's mysteries, with power to bind and to loose 'in
the person of Christ,' its members fellow-citizens with
the saints and of the household of God, heirs of a
long line of heroes, who by faith overcame the world.
In contrast with that world which lies around it, the
Church of Christ claims to be the kingdom of life
and light and love; its life quickening, its light
irradiating, its love transforming all that is brought
within its reach. It boasts that it is the fount of
every human virtue, the channel of supernatural
graces, the custodian of truth, the regenerator of
man ; the one all-embracing unity which, without
destroying the natural character of human life, yet
lifts it into the life of God. It claims the right to
speak and to be heard in all matters, for it recognises
no region of human life or thought as lying outside
its pale. Claiming all, it is greater than all. Recognising all, it by recognising raises all. It touches
the moral life of the individual, not merely by setting
before him a nobler and truer ideal, but by imparting
to his nature new powers to enable him to realise it.
It touches family life, giving as it were its *imprimatur*

G

to filial obedience and brotherly love, and lifting the
highest and yet most natural of earthly unions, the
marriage relation, to the level of a sacramental
ordinance. It enters into social and political life,
giving a Divine sanction to the great principles of law
and order and obedience, and yet securing to the
world—in the only sense in which those often misused terms can have permanent and abiding value—
Freedom, Equality, and Brotherhood in the light of
the Incarnation and the Fatherhood of God.

It is little wonder that a religion which makes
such transcendent claims should be met by the
question, 'By what authority?' 'Who gave Thee
this authority?' The question is uttered in every
tone. It is whispered anxiously and earnestly by
the disciple who fain would justify the faith he holds
before those who hold it not. It is heard in the
arrogant and defiant challenge of those for whom
the Christian revelation has come to be but an in-
teresting field for antiquarian research, and Christian
faith a natural object of ridicule and contempt.

In such days every Christian becomes an apologist,
an apologist as well as a missionary, though our
apologies like our missionary efforts sometimes show
more zeal than wisdom. What then can we learn
from Christ's own answer to the challenge, 'By what
authority doest Thou these things?'

And the first thing we notice is that Christ answers
not only by a proof but by an appeal; an appeal too
which found no response in the hearts of those
who challenged Him. They did not believe in the

supernatural mission of the Baptist, whatever the people thought. But they feared the people they despised. They dared not say that John Baptist had no Divine mission : they would not confess that his mission was from God. Hence they were silenced, but not convinced. But with the people it was different. They believed that John was 'a prophet indeed,' and in recognising the prophetic character of John's message they had already recognised an authority speaking in man yet coming from God. For though the Baptist spoke with authority and rebuked with power, his authority and power were derived and not inherent. It was so by his own confession. Men came to him with the question, 'Who art thou?' And he answered, ' I am a voice, a messenger, a forerunner. Repent, prepare, make ready. The Kingdom of God is at hand.' And presently in more definite, yet more mysterious tones, he speaks :— 'There is One among you Whom ye know not. He is mightier than I. His shoe's latchet I am not worthy to stoop down and unloose. He must increase, I must decrease, as the reflected light of the moon must pale before the rising sun. My work is the βάπτισμα εἰς μετάνοιαν ; His the λουτρὸν παλιγγενεσίας. I preach repentance ; He absolves. I prepare the way for Christ, "Behold the Lamb of God, Who taketh away the sins of the world." '

The question then which silenced the Pharisees, while it left them unconvinced, was to those who believed in John an adequate reply. It was an appeal to their reason through their faith, not an

appeal to their faith through their reason. Here
surely we touch a great principle. We can only
prove the truth of anything to a man by means of
that which he already holds. Men still talk of
proving Christianity by miracles, forgetting the some-
what obvious truth that a miracle can be evidence of
nothing to one who denies that the miracle is a fact.
For those who witnessed the miracles it was a valid and
convincing argument. In answer to John Baptist's
question Christ said, 'Go and show John again those
things which ye do hear and see : the blind receive
their sight, and the lame walk, the lepers are cleansed,
and the deaf hear, the dead are raised up, and the
poor have the Gospel preached to them.' All these
wonders—and the last is a climax, not a bathos—
were accepted facts, and therefore could be appealed
to as evidence. But it is different now. Miracles in
the moral world—souls converted, lives transformed,
selfishness overcome by a word from the Cross—
these we see around us every day. To them we may
appeal. But the great miracles of the past, even
that greatest of all miracles, the Resurrection of Jesus
Christ, cannot be put in the forefront of an apology
to those who question the fact or the possibility of
miracles. To what then can we appeal? Shall we
appeal to prophecy if not to miracle? Criticism, real
and so-called, has here a store of difficulties as great
as any which science can bring against miracles.
And if we sometimes feel that in the background
there lies an *a priori* assumption that prophecy is impossible, yet a mass of critical learning appears in

the foreground to prove that in a given case the prophecy was after the fact.

We are driven back then more and more upon the character of Christ and the actual power of Christianity to transform life and regenerate nature. Miracles and prophecy are still for the Christian what they have always been, but in dealing with those who reject them we find ourselves brought back to the crucial question, 'What think ye of Christ?' and this again falls back upon a further question : What think ye of Conscience? For to ask, 'What think ye of Christ?' is to appeal to the Conscience, and such an appeal can find no response in those who refuse to recognise its unique, its paramount authority.

When, then, men challenge Christianity to prove its right over life and conduct, when the Church is met by the hostile challenge, 'By what authority doest thou these things? and who gave thee this authority?'—she is only adopting her Lord's method when she replies by a question and an appeal :—

The authority of Conscience, is it from Heaven, or of men?

On the answer given to that question the whole case for Christianity turns. Destroy Conscience, deny its power, shut your ears to its warnings, or explain them away, and you have implicitly rejected Him Who speaks in it. Miracles and Prophecy, the Inspired Word, the Church's faith—these will no longer help you. But reverence Conscience, listen to it, obey its slightest hint, and already ye have prepared the way for Christ, Whose messenger it is.

The parallel here is very close. (1) The message
of the Baptist was in time prior to the teaching of
Christ.  It prepared the way.  And yet its explanation, its ultimate justification, is to be found in the
Advent of the Messiah.  Apart from that it was
incomplete and meaningless.  For the authority of
the messenger was derived from Him Who 'coming
after was preferred before' him.  So Conscience, the
*lumen naturale*, which speaks in man and yet is not
of man, which has been called 'the creative principle
of religion,' finds its explanation and its justification
in the doctrine of the Incarnation, and derives its
authority from Him Who is Judge of quick and
dead.

Again, (2) Conscience speaks to those who will
listen to it in a voice of stern rebuke.  It tells not
only of an ideal unrealised, but of a broken law, of
guilt incurred, of a judgment present and to come.
It almost terrifies us by its command.  Its 'categorical
imperative' seems hard, and stern, and cruel, when
we have realised our moral weakness.  We look
backward, and it makes cowards of us ; we look forward, and it paralyses us.  It is like the warning
'Repent ye' of the Baptist.  And yet in its very
sternness it leads us on.  Like the Law given amid
the thunders of Sinai, it is a παιδαγωγὸς εἰς Χριστόν.
The Revelation of Christ 'republishes' that truth of
natural religion, the eternal distinction between good
and evil, between light and darkness, between 'the
law, which is holy, and just, and good,' and the natural
man, 'carnal, sold under sin.'  But it does more than

republish. For Christianity is not, as the last-century deist affirmed, 'as old as creation.' It gives that which Conscience cannot give, a washing of regeneration, a new nature, a new life. And as that new nature, that new life, overcomes the old, the sternness of Conscience disappears. The new life increases, the old law decreases. There is no formal unreal imputation, no immoral forensic fiction, but a real triumph of life over death in man himself, till the Christian dares to say, 'Who will bring any charge against them whom God has made righteous?' Who is he that will condemn when Christ the Judge absolves?

As then the acceptance or rejection of the authority of Christ depended for the Jews of His day on the view they adopted of John's baptism, so for us the question of the claims of Christ must ultimately be determined by the view we take of Conscience. Is it from Heaven, or of men? Is its judgment valid? its authority without appeal? its decision irrevocable? Faith in God and faith in duty, if they do not always go hand in hand, are closely connected. In days when a consistently selfish theory of morals was possible we are not surprised to find religion recommended as a paying speculation, or at least as a reasonably safe investment. Nor was it strange that Christianity could be conceived of as 'a comfortable, middle-class, soul-saving system.' But those days are not ours. Our age with all its faults is earnest, and would be moral. There is self-sacrifice, benevolence, enthusiasm, within and without the pale of the Christian Church. And yet probably the contrast was never more marked than now between faith and doubt. Many profess to obey the dictates of Conscience, but they no longer recognise in it the voice of God. Hence when Christianity advances its claims to authority, and challenges submission, they answer with the question—By what authority, and who gave you that authority? The moral beauty of Christ's character men readily admit,—its attractiveness as an ideal, its purity, its unselfishness, its unworldliness. But its sterner side, its unique claim upon the Conscience itself, its absolute supremacy in the moral world,—this they shrink from allowing.

And if we ask, ' Why is this ?' we can hardly conceal from ourselves the fact that Conscience has lost in authority as it has ceased to be mysterious. Men talk as if at last Conscience had been *found out.* They know its origin, they can trace its development, they have found its analogue in the brute. What is it but a natural instinct immeasurably refined ? or an elaborately specialised organ for estimating utility or measuring the volume of life ? How can we any longer speak of it as a voice from Heaven, or conceive of it as endowed with supernatural authority, or make it a guarantee for the existence of God, or appeal to it in support of His Revelation in Christ ?

Such reasoning,—and it is common enough nowadays,—would be illogical enough if it stood alone. But it does not. It is the last phase in a long controversy, and is intelligible only in the light of that

controversy. Well-meaning but ill-advised defenders
of Conscience have often based its authority on the
fact that it has no history. They have spoken of it
as a sort of Melchizedek in the moral world, 'without
father, without mother, and without descent,' appear-
ing full grown upon the scene, and claiming the
homage due to royalty. And their opponents have
readily accepted the test so unwisely proposed, and
now that they think they have discovered the origin of
Conscience they feel justified in setting its authority
aside. The argument is strangely like that used by
the men of Nazareth to invalidate the claims of
Christ. ' Is not this,' they said, ' the carpenter's son,
whose father and mother we know ? ' 'When Christ
cometh no man knoweth whence He is.' And so because they had seen Him growing up amongst them,
and knew the truth of His humanity, they denied
that He was very God.

Yet the question of the validity of a faculty is
distinct from the question of its origin. What we call
reason is the consciousness of truth, what we call
conscience is the consciousness of right. It is con-
ceivable that both reason and conscience may some
day be traced back to an origin which seems to us now
unworthy of their present greatness, yet the question
of their validity, the real correspondence of the
faculty with its object, the power of reason to give us
truth, of conscience to unfold the law of right, is left
untouched. The strength of manhood is what it is,
though it grew out of the helplessness of infancy. It
is only in the moral region that men commit

themselves to the paradox that Conscience is not Conscience because it has a history.

And yet, brethren, paradoxical as such a view may
seem, it is a great and real danger. The whole stress
and drift of what is evil in us is against the claims of
Conscience. We are always trying to invalidate its
judgments, or excuse ourselves from obedience, to
legislate for ourselves as exceptional cases, and little
by little to withdraw ourselves from its control. And
it comes to us as a new discovery in our day, that we
can analyse Conscience away, and having, as we think,
traced it to its source, we can safely deny its authority.
As a faculty for measuring pleasures and pains we can
indeed justify its existence, but as such it has only
conditional authority. We cannot reverence it, we
cannot trust it always, we cannot see in it the messenger
of God speaking to us from Him. It is robbed of its
supernatural power. And at the same time human
life has been degraded to a lower level. It has lost
its direct and immediate contact with the spiritual
world, with God Himself. We no longer know ourselves, our human nature, as the meeting-point of two
worlds, and so, imperceptibly at first, we fall out of
correspondence with the unseen, and find ourselves at
last face to face with the question, Is God knowable?
And the question carries with it its own negation, as
surely as the challenge of the Pharisee was a denial of
the authority of Christ.

On the other hand, to admit the authority of Conscience, and to suffer it to regulate life, is already to
have gone far to recognise Christ Himself. ‘ He that

receiveth whomsoever I send,' said Christ, 'receiveth Me.' 'If these things be in you, and abound,' says S. Peter, speaking of the most unselfish of the moral virtues, 'they make you that ye shall neither be barren nor unfruitful in the knowledge of our Lord Jesus Christ.' The disinterested reverence for right is an implicit recognition of the claims of Him Who is the Righteousness of God, even as the generous love of goodness is implicitly a love of God.

Is Conscience then from Heaven, or of man ? That is the great question of our day, the question which really lies behind, and is preliminary to that other question, What think ye of Christ ? For Christianity is from the first an appeal to the Conscience, and according to the purity and strength of Conscience will the clearness of its answer be. Where the appeal to the Conscience finds no response, prophecy and miracle will have no force. 'If they hear not Moses and the Prophets, neither will they be persuaded though one rose from the dead.' The Pharisees had Moses and the Prophets, and appealed to them against Him 'of Whom Moses in the Law and the Prophets did write.' They had the witness of the Baptist, and resisted its claim lest it should lead them on to admit the authority of Christ. What wonder that when they saw Christ's miracles they put them also aside ! 'Give God the praise, we know that this man is a sinner.' 'He casteth out devils through Beelzebub, the prince of the devils.' Anything rather than allow the authoritative claim of Him Who said, 'For judgment I am come into this world.'

My brothers, the forces of our day are concentrating themselves upon that which God has given to man to be the witness of Himself, the natural light which is an earnest of a supernatural grace. Popular theories, miscalled scientific, tend to undermine its authority ; criticism, so called, has confused men's minds, and shaken their faith in that which, more than all that we have inherited from the Greeks, has been the real educator of the Conscience,—the Inspired Word of God. A cynicism, which appeals to us most strongly in our weakest moments, tends to draw down to a lower level the highest actions, or to read into them a selfish aim. And the tendency of all is to make us believe that Conscience is not 'from Heaven' but 'of men.' And yet in such an atmosphere men presume to discuss the claim of Christianity, and challenge its authority. And others wonder that the atrophy of conscience is followed by the atrophy of faith. Those were wise far-reaching words which closed a well-known address by one whom Oxford long will honour,—the late Professor Green. 'Faith in God and duty will survive much doubt and difficulty and distress, and perhaps attain to some nobler mode of itself under their influence. But if once we have come to acquiesce in such a standard of living as must make us wish God and duty to be illusions, it must surely die.' 'You cannot find a verification of the idea of God and duty ; you can only make it.'

Come what may then, brethren, be loyal and true to what is noblest in you, like him who 'reverenced his conscience as his king.' Be on your guard against the temptation to interpret the acts of others by the least worthy motive. It is more than ungenerous. It deals a deadly blow at Conscience itself. Accustom yourselves to believe that others, even when you least agree with them, are trying to 'do God service,' and that, if conscientiousness is not always truth, at least it is a condition without which truth cannot be. So doing, you will learn to reverence Conscience in yourself, and hear in it the voice of God. So doing, you will honour Him in Whose Name and by Whose authority Conscience speaks, Whose messenger and forerunner Conscience claims to be, Who, as the rational unity of all that is, is the object of philosophy, in Whom, as the Personal Object of religious worship, Conscience beholds its sovereign God.

# IV.

## THE POWER OF CHRIST
## IN THE MORAL LIFE.

'His word was with power.'—S. LUKE iv. 32.

OUR Lord not only claimed to speak with authority, 'His word was with power.' Behind His claim to authority men felt that there was that which justified His claim. 'All power,' He said, 'is given unto Me in heaven and in earth'; power 'to heal sicknesses' and remove physical evil; 'power against unclean spirits, to cast them out'; 'power to forgive sins' as only God forgives, and to bid the poor fallen sinner to 'go, and sin no more.' Whether in the physical or the moral world, Christ claimed to speak with authority; and 'His word was with power.'

Judged, at least, by those among whom He lived and wrought, His claim justified itself in that region, where a pretended authority would most easily be found out. Evil spirits recognised His voice. With authority and power He commanded, and they obeyed. If men question His power in the moral world, His power to forgive sins, Christ refers them to that which is open to the eyes of men. 'Whether is easier to say, Thy sins be forgiven thee, or to say, Arise and walk? But that ye may know that the Son of Man hath power on earth to forgive sins, then saith He unto the sick of the palsy, Arise, and take up thy bed, and go unto thy house.'

Thus by proving His power in the world of nature, Christ prepared the minds of the Jews to believe in His power in the moral world. With us it is necessarily different. We have exchanged the naïvely objective attitude of ancient thought for the distrustful introspectiveness of modern days. And it is easier for us to believe in miracles on the strength of what we know of Christ's power in the moral world, than to base our faith in that power on the evidence of miracles. We must begin with what is nearest to us. And the present power of Christ in the moral life is nearer to each one of us than the miracles which witnessed to that power in days of old.

When, however, we claim for Christ and Christianity power in the moral world, we notice that there is a sense in which the claim is generally admitted. Christian morality has won its way to a secure position. Men, who are far enough from accepting the Christian faith, will in most cases admit the Sermon on the Mount to an unique place in the history of ethics. Whatever views may be held as to the Teacher Himself, it is generally, if not always, conceded that His moral teaching is without a rival. As the highest known ideal of character, it appeals to the Conscience, and Conscience recognises its superiority. Indeed, if Christianity meant only the publication of certain high moral principles, it might reckon on few open enemies.

But, in truth, Christianity, like the Sermon on the Mount itself, means much more than this. Had Christianity been merely the introduction into the world of a new and higher moral ideal than men had known, had it even presented us only with a view of human character which after ages would recognise as final and complete, it would have been, as it were, in the same plane with other moral ideals, differing from them in degree, but not in kind, standing supreme above them only in its universality and permanence, as the perfect character of man as man. But such an ideal would paralyse, not inspire, effort. The more true, the more perfect it was, the more hopelessly would it seem beyond the reach of the ordinary man. Imagine to yourselves the Christian ideal, with its utter unselfishness, its unworldliness, its universal benevolence, its self-renunciation, its humility, its purity, revealed to the world, which witnessed its first proclamation, as an end to be aimed at, not by philosophers or saints, but by all mankind, as the true human life. Does not our knowledge of human nature enable us to forecast the result? The philosophical moralist passes by on the other side; it is οὐ πρακτὸν οὐδὲ κτητὸν ἀνθρώπῳ;[1] and the saint, who knows more fully than any the reality of moral evil, the weakness of man's effort after good, turns away in despair. I was alive once, but now that I have seen the vision of the holy

---

[1] Aristotle, *Ethics*, i. iv.

and just and pure, I feel, as I never felt till now, the weight of this body of death. And what is the appeal of such a character to the ordinary man? It is so far above him and beyond him ; it implies such a reversal of his own life and the lives of others, as he is wont to see them around him, that it seems impossible, a mere visionary's dream, like the picture of a golden age expressing merely the obverse of things as they really are. And

> ' Who can hold a fire in his hand,
> By thinking on the frosty Caucasus?
> Or cloy the hungry edge of appetite,
> By bare imagination of a feast?
> Or wallow naked in December snow,
> By thinking on fantastic summer's heat?'

This impracticability of the Christian ideal is plainly admitted in the latest attack on Christianity, the most significant attack, perhaps, of recent years. We are told that 'this pursuit of a spirituality utterly beyond attainment by ordinary mortals, beautiful as it is when attained, operates injuriously on the morality of average men and women. The standard proposed is so exalted that instead of attracting the ordinary person to aim at reaching it, it discourages and repels him. He is inwardly conscious that he cannot possibly reach it, even if he tries ever so much.'[1]

This is a remarkable admission. Time was when it was said : 'We accept your Christian morality, we recognise the perfection of its moral ideal, but supernaturalism, dogma, priesthood, and sacraments, these

J. C. Morison, *The Service of Man*, cap. vii.

II

we can do without.' And when the Christian dared to suggest that there is no sure foundation for the Christian virtues but the Christian verities, he was accused of undermining morality by making it dependent on religion. And now we are openly told, by one who has himself abandoned the Christian faith, and believes that the age is abandoning it too, that the Christian moral ideal is too exalted, and that people are 'deterred from embracing a serious view of life's duties, just because a standard of such exalted perfection is proposed to them that they know it is of no use attempting to reach it.'

It is something for us to have learned from such a source the close connection of the Christian faith with the Christian life; to be reminded that the Christian ideal, treated merely as an ideal, and apart from that supernatural grace whereby it was to be realised, would, for the great mass of men, paralyse rather than stimulate moral effort. It would sound to them like mockery to say, 'Be holy, be pure, be humble, sacrifice self, live for others,' if that command did not come from one who could give them the power to obey.

But Christ's word was with power. He never said to the starved souls, 'Depart in peace, be ye warmed and filled,' without giving them that which they had sought in vain. He never said to the paralysed cripple, 'Arise and walk,' without giving new strength to the feeble limbs. 'Thy sins be forgiven thee' was neither a forensic fiction, nor a charitable hypothesis, nor the kindly expression of a benevolent wish. 'His word was with power.' If it had not been so, Christ might have been a teacher still, a pattern still, but not a Saviour. It would have been true to say of the Gospel, as S. Augustine says of the Law, as we may say of all non-Christian ethical systems, *jubere tantum non adjuvare poterant.*[1] But Christ's word was with power, and it was the consciousness of this that enabled the first Christians, with all their knowledge of human weakness and moral evil, to aim so high, and yet to go forward so hopefully, so triumphantly, to the struggle.

And if we ask in what the power of Christianity lay, as distinct from the authority which a high and pure ideal exercises over the conscience, we find that —First, it placed the Christian in organic relation with a higher and supernatural life. Nothing could have brought the high ideal of Christianity within the region of practical effort for the ordinary man, but the belief that a new power had entered into human nature, and that man had become something different from what, in sad experience, he knew himself to be. 'Teach a man,' it is said, 'that he is something greater than he is, and he will soon come to be what he believes himself to be.' Christianity did not merely teach men that they were greater than they thought; it claimed to make human nature greater than it had been. As Jews, the first Christians were familiar with the thought of a people singled out to a kind of priesthood among the nations, brought near to God, and intrusted with His oracles, that through them He might educate the world.

[1] *De Peccatorum Meritis et Remissione,* I. xi. 13.

But that old idea would not contain the wider truth,
the larger hope of Christianity. So the new wine
burst the bottle. Jewish exclusiveness must be
abandoned, if the world is to receive the idea of the
redemption of man as man, through Him in Whom
differences of Jew and Gentile, male and female, bar-
barian and civilised, disappear, because He is the
perfect Man. That notion of the universality of
Christianity, though but slowly realised by the first
disciples, is yet implicit in Christ's own teaching;
and the Incarnation, both in the order of time and
in the order of thought, is the ground of the belief
in the brotherhood of man, as it is the justification
for that 'enthusiasm of humanity,' which has become
a catch-word of the day. And the sure hope which
carried the Christian forward was a supernatural hope.
Chosen out of the world, the object of the world's
hatred and persecution, he was yet, as he believed,
in the purpose of God, the world's conqueror. By
the mere fact of his being a Christian, he was (if we
may use such a phrase), on the winning side in the
great moral struggle between light and darkness.
The future was with him. For a moment his faith
might fail, when Christ, the embodiment of all his
triumphant expectation, died upon the cross. But
with the new assurance of the Resurrection, the new
Presence of Whitsunday, he went forth fearlessly to
overcome the world, the forces of evil within him and
around him, knowing that he was endued with power
from on high, for the regeneration of man.

Judged by human standards, nothing could have

been more fanatical than this attempt. A few hundred, at the most, without learning, without influence, debarred from the use of the world's weapons, they went out to obey their Lord's command, 'Go ye into all the world, and preach the Gospel to every creature.' They knew that 'His word was with power,' that the 'I ought' implied the 'I can,' and in the faith of that supernatural power which was theirs they went forth to the struggle. 'Be of good cheer,' their Lord had said, 'I have overcome the world.' And when, as He had foretold, there came upon them 'tribulation, or distress, or famine, or nakedness, or peril, or the sword,' the Christian fearlessly declared, 'In all these things we are more than conquerors, through Him that loved us.'

It is hard for us even to understand the immediateness of the presence of the supernatural world to the early Christian Church. Those words of the Jerusalem Council, 'It seemed good to the Holy Ghost, and to us,' imply a certainty of Divine direction, which in a later age would seem almost profane. 'Who art thou?' said the Emperor to S. Ignatius, —'Who art thou who dost disobey our orders, and leadest others to disobey?' And the answer is, 'I am Theophorus, the God-bearer, for I carry Christ within me.'[1] It is not to our present purpose to speak of the means by which the living union with God was secured by prayer and sacrament. Certainly, it never occurred to the first Christians to regard Sacraments as religious luxuries, for those who

---

[1] Martyrdom of St. Ignatius, *Antiochene Acts*, § 2.

aspired to something more than the ordinary Christian life. They were the normal channels by which that new life flowed into their souls; they were not ecclesiastical ordinances, as men sometimes think of them now, but moral instruments, having their natural and necessary place in the moral life. The Christian conception of moral evil is unintelligible apart from this belief in the immediate relation with the supernatural. That 'horror of sin' which a recent historian of ethics speaks of as characteristic of Christianity, arose from the belief that moral defilement separated from the supernatural life, and broke the contact with the Divine society in which the life of Christ was realised.

(ii.) But it was not merely to the belief in a presence with them of a supernatural life that Christianity owed its power. The Divine touched the human in an intensely personal relationship.

We see this most plainly in that virtue, in which the Christian stood most opposed to the heathen world, the virtue of purity. Here, more than in either of the other parts of temperance, Christianity was committed to an ideal, unknown and unintelligible to heathen morals. We know how the controversy with heathen impurity showed itself in the early days of the Church. What were the weapons which the Christian teacher used? What was his appeal? We have been told of late years that 'there is no true foundation for the strictest sexual morality other than the social duty which the Greeks asserted.'[1] Did, then, the Christian teacher appeal to social

[1] T. II. Green, *Prolegomena to Ethics*, p. 287.

duty? Did he appeal, as we might now, to reverence
for human personality? to a chivalrous respect for
womanhood? to the theoretical, if not actual,
equality of all members in the body politic? There
is not one word of this, nor could there be, for as
yet there was, outside the Christian Church, no recognition of humanity as a family with equal rights.
What, then, is his appeal? It is direct, personal,
immediate. ' What! know ye not that your body is
the temple of the Holy Ghost Which is in you, Which
ye have of God, and ye are not your own?' 'Know
ye not that your bodies are the members of Christ?
Shall I then take the members of Christ, and make
them the members of an harlot? God forbid!'

Even those relationships which to many in the
present day seem to begin and end with man—to be
simply relations between man and man—were for the
Christian taken up into his personal devotion to
Christ. There were not for him two kinds of love,
love to God and love to man. Charity was always
a theological virtue, it was love of God, and of our
neighbour in God. It was that personal relation of
the Christian with God in Christ which saved his
service of God from melting away into a dreamy
pantheism, and his service of man from being dissipated into a generalised feeling of benevolence. The
Master had said, ' Inasmuch as ye have done it unto
one of the least of these My brethren, ye have done it
unto Me.' And the disciple was quick to interpret the
thought. If Christ gave up His life for us, we ought
also to give up our lives for the brethren. Such a

necessary consequence is it that S. John fearlessly
argues from the effect to the cause : 'We know that
we have passed from death unto life, because we love
the brethren.'    And 'He that loveth not his brother
whom he hath seen, how can he love God Whom he
hath not seen ?'

Thus, in his devotion to the service of man, no less
than in his efforts to attain to holiness and purity in
himself, the same power of personal appeal was present with him.    Who of us has not felt, in the rush
of temptation, the strength and help of human sympathy just when our feet were almost gone.    For the
Christian, the sympathy of Christ was more than this.
It was human, yet Divine.    It was as strong as it was
tender.    It transformed, even while it stimulated, the
Christian's effort.    No victory to which that voice
summoned him in the world within or the world
without was too great for him to achieve.    'I can do
all things through Christ Which strengtheneth me.'

(iii.) But once more the power of Christianity in
the moral life consisted not only in the gift of supernatural strength, and the tenderness of a personal
appeal, but in the fact that it dealt with man as a
social being.    His regeneration was to be in and
through a society—a society not of this world, for its
laws, its methods, its conditions of membership, were
other than those with which the world was familiar.
In his relation with God man stands alone.    Alone,
in the awful isolation of his personal responsibility,
he must face death and judgment.    'No man may
deliver his brother nor make agreement unto God

for him. He must let that alone for ever.'[1] But the present age does not need to be reminded that man's nature is social, that he has necessary relations with others, that his individual life is fully realised only in relation with these, and that to seek to stand alone is to declare one's-self ἢ θηρίον ἢ Θεός,[2] greater or less than man. Hence, Christianity is not cast upon the world to triumph by its own intrinsic truth and beauty. Nor are individuals, as individuals, drawn to Christ without relation to their fellow-men. The Christianity of Christ is truer to human nature than the Christianity of many Christians. For if we honestly ask ourselves, How did Christ will to give to humanity the salvation which He had wrought for it? we are bound to answer, whatever our prejudices may be, He did not write a book; He did not formulate a creed; He founded a society. He selected and trained its first members for the work they were to do, and then sent them forth to gather into the spiritual kingdom, by the power of personal influence, those who were far off, as well as those who were near, 'Baptizing them in the Name of the Father and of the Son and of the Holy Ghost.'

In these days we spend so much anxious thought on the development of the Church that we are tempted to lose sight of this primary fact. Some, through fear of the mediæval view of unity, and still more of the mediæval methods of securing it, have almost persuaded themselves that the idea of a visible society originated in the brain of S. Augustine,

---

[1] Psalm xlix. 7, 8 (Psalter).  [2] Arist. *Pol.* i. 2. 14.

as the result of his controversy with the Donatists.
Others who have realised the fact that the spiritual
organism was not made, but grew, have been led away
by the verbal argument, and, applying to it biological methods, have tried to treat structure apart from
function, while a microscopic antiquarianism is offered
to us as a kind of ecclesiastical histology.

But all these questions, as to what is permanent
and what is transient in the organisation of the
Church, serve to throw into the shade the fact which
lies behind them all—the fact, namely, that the
Christian, just because he is a Christian, is a member
of a spiritual society, of which Holy Baptism is the
initiatory rite, the Eucharist the living bond of union,
while its Magna Charta is the Sermon on the Mount.
In the early days of Christianity there were no
Christians unattached. But the sixteenth-century revolt from the view which had been stereotyped by
the mediæval Church led by a natural reaction, in
our own country especially, to a pronounced individualism from which we are but slowly recovering.
An atomistic and mechanical theory of nature, the
result of Cartesian and Baconian physics, had its
reflex in a sophistic theory of the State, surmounted,
and for a moment neutralised, by the belief in the
Divine right of kings. On this day,[1] of all days in
the year, we need not be reminded of the fatal consequences of that theory in the region of politics, nor
need we be surprised to find the Church struggling in
vain in defence of the true view of what a society is,

---

[1] January 30, the Anniversary of the Death of Charles I.

and falling back at last upon a religious individualism, thinly disguised under the sacred name of personal religion ; while outside the Established Church the individualistic principle was openly recognised, and the numberless religious sects are the result.

Slowly in the present day we are recovering the truth that the Church is a society, not a federation ; an organic growth, not a voluntary concourse of religious atoms : that it exists, in the purpose of Him Who founded it, to be a moral instrument for the development in the individual man of the Christ-like character, for the transformation of human nature into that which is Divine.

My brothers, the question which, in this day, we are called upon to answer is this : Can we sustain the Christlike character, can it even be to us a possible ideal, if we no longer believe in the power which in the past has wrought out that character in saints and heroes ? That power, we have seen, consists in the consciousness of a supernatural Presence in us ; in the personal relation of man with God in Christ ; in the knowledge that we have communion and fellowship one with another in the Divine Society.

Can we, in the old age of the world, dispense with these ? Will the momentum derived from a faith, which was once real to us, carry us on through that period of moral interregnum which, we are told, must precede the establishment of morals on a physical basis ? There are those who confidently answer in the affirmative. And yet, perhaps, the most striking feature of the thought of our age is the sadness and

the gloom which is settling down upon us. Is it an
accident that it synchronises so strangely with the
loss of faith? that the men who are most sure that
the world has outgrown the belief in God are most
instant in prophetic warnings of coming evil, most
convinced that pessimism is the only reasoned conclusion from the facts? It seems as if the age were
losing hope in proportion as it loses its faith. How
long will charity, the third in the trinity of theological
virtues, survive the rest? It is an assumption which
we have no right to make, that lives of heroic self-
sacrifice for others, like those of Margaret Hallahan,
Sister Agnes Jones, and Sister Dora, would have
been what they were, if they had not been lived in
the power of faith and hope and love.

And if we cannot spare that belief in a supernatural presence as a power working with us and in
us, as little can we afford to lose the power which
comes from the personal relation of man with God
in Christ. 'We live by admiration, hope, and love,'
and these demand a personal object. As against any
system which men, with a true instinct, stamp as
mere ecclesiasticism, we appeal to the immediate
personal relationship of the individual soul with God,
a relationship made real and perfect by prayer and
communing with Him. We appeal to it as giving
power and confidence and hope to man, enabling him
to fight in the spirit of a conqueror though he were
alone against the world.

And yet we dare to go beyond the point of view
of those to whom the existence of a visible Church

seems to imply the limiting or the destruction of personal religion. We cannot thus set brotherhood against freedom, any more than we can think of the State as the limiting rather than the expression of rights. And therefore we dare to claim that the power which Christ gave for the salvation of humanity, implied, not as an accident but as an essential, a real communion of man with man in a Divine Society, a *Civitas Dei*, which is not opposed to, but includes, a *Regnum Hominis.* And if in this we differ from those who are fighting nobly side by side with us in the conflict against moral evil, it is because we believe that to maintain the doctrine of a Holy Catholic Church is to be true to the purpose of Christ, true to human nature, true to the idea of brotherhood.

There are those who will tell us that these things are not a source of power but of weakness in the moral life. Christianity is nowadays summoned to Canossa by the Hildebrand of non-Christian dogmatism. We are told that supernaturalism leads men to be careless of the duties of their life in the world, that personal religion easily becomes selfish, and therefore un-Christian, that the history of the Church is the record of intolerance and bigotry and exclusiveness, and not of brotherhood.

How much of truth or falsehood there is in these charges we need not now stay to inquire. In the face of history we dare not deny that Christianity has fallen very far short of the purpose of its Lord. We know, too, that in the strife of warring creeds the final victory must rest with that which, whether it finds its motive in the love of God, or solely in the service of man, yet manifests itself in the truest, the most real, most Christlike human character.

And knowing this, Christianity does not shrink from the trial. Amid the gloom of a despairing age, it dares to speak still with hope and confidence. The shadows of doubt and sadness close round us now and again. In our personal struggles with evil, or in our efforts to work for God, there comes upon us a great weariness; we are ready to fold our hands and let things go. Is it any use struggling? Must I not adopt a lower standard for myself and for others? Has not science shown me that by heredity my character is made for me at birth? Are not the laws of human development as fixed as the laws of nature? I look out into the world, and I am ready to say with the prophet in Horeb, 'I only am left.' Lord, they pull down Thine altars, they reject Thy truth, they will not receive the revelation of Thy Son. And the answer comes, What doest thou here? Is it a time for solitude, and separation, and intro-spection, when so much work for God is to be done? 'God is faithful. He will not suffer you to be tempted above that ye are able.' Temptation conquers a man only so far as he yields to it. Go back to the struggle. Do some little work for man; win some victory for God; claim all that is good and true in human life as belonging of right to Christ. Go in a strength which is not your own to the battle which is the Lord's. It is enough that you have the command and the promise of Him Whose word is with power.

# V.

## THE PRESENCE OF GOD
## IN THE CHRISTIAN AND THE CHURCH.

'And He said, My presence shall go with thee, and I will give thee rest. And he said unto Him, If Thy presence be not with me, carry us not up hence.'—EXODUS xxxiii. 14, 15.

'GOD,' it has been said, 'by nature alike and by grace, makes new beginnings the whole history of our being.' 'New beginnings are the life of perseverance, though they seem at first sight contradictory to it, or to presuppose its absence or suspension.' In the world in which we live day and night succeed one another, seed-time and harvest, summer and winter. In nature, as in grace, God's compassions fail not; they are new every morning.

> 'New every morning is the love,
> Our wakening and uprising prove,
> From sleep and darkness safely brought,
> Restored to life, and power, and thought.
>
> New mercies each returning day,
> Hover around us while we pray,
> New perils past, new sins forgiven,
> New thoughts of God, new hopes of heaven.'

It is a familiar truth to us, in the case of our bodily life, that constant renewal, that daily and hourly

repairing of the waste that is going on; that inter-
action of forces, chemical and vital, by which our
bodies, so long as life lasts, are ever changing, while
the citadel of personality is still untouched. For all
through these changes of growth we are still the same;
character is slowly forming for good or ill, and we are
responsible to God and to our fellow-men for what we
do, and what we think, and what we are. Childhood
has given way to youth, and youth to manhood, and
manhood (if it please God) will melt into old age; but
these are but phases, and we know it in a continuous
life, which in its completeness is *our* life. We look
back over it and mark its epochs, its turning-points,
its new departures—they are parts of one whole, links
in one unbroken chain. Such is life as we look back
upon it from the end, and see it in its true perspective.

But while we are living our life we do not fully
realise this continuity. Each new epoch seems like
a breach with what has gone before, and we shrink
from it or welcome it, according to our dispositions or
our age. What strikes us most forcibly is the contrast
between the new and the old. And in the buoyancy
of youthful hope we welcome every change. 'Ring
out the false, ring in the true.' The new, it seems to
us, must be better than the old. We must be entering on a nobler, purer, stronger life than that which
is passing away. The old school-days, with their
brightness and their dark stains, are gone to God.
University life opens upon us. It is a new beginning,
and seems so full of promise. And then the happy
time up here passes all too quickly, and we stand, as so

many of us are standing now, on the threshold of a
new life. The Summer term, for many of our friends,
if not for ourselves, means the end of the protected
years. A few weeks, and we must face the great
issues of life in the open world, and play our several
parts for God. And we know that we shall look back
to the old Oxford days, and wonder we did not prize
them more and use them better for gathering the
strength for the coming years.

But as time rolls on, and other changes come, we
meet them less hopefully. There is more of sadness
in the contrast between the old and the new. We
are more conscious of failure and disappointment
in the past, less joyous and hopeful for the future.
We are more ready than we once were to listen to the
sad judgment of those who tell us that 'youth is a
delusion, manhood a struggle, old age a regret.' We
look back, and the days of a long life seem 'few and
evil,' a series of broken resolutions, bright dreams
scattered, youthful hopes unrealised, change and
decay everywhere, sorrow, suffering, sickness, failing
powers, life a monotonous conflict against nature with
the certainty of being vanquished at the last—so little
done, so much left undone. Surely it is not worth
living.

Such a view of life is not natural to the young, and
yet just in proportion as the consciousness of God's
Presence has faded out of men's belief, it has become
common even for them. The sadness of life is indeed
almost a fashionable theme, and, when all due allow-
ance has been made for fashion, the fact remains that

we are sadder than our fathers, more given to in-
trospection, less hopeful for the future, less sure and
definite in our faith, less steady and consistent in the
conduct of our lives.　We cannot be enthusiastic
about life if it may be only a series of attempts fore-
doomed to failure, if we cannot see in it a unity, a
continuity, a purpose, which is realised in and by our
failures and our new beginnings.

What then is it which can give this unity and
continuity to life, which will enable us to trace in all
its changes a growth and progress analogous to that
which runs through the changes of our physical nature?
The answer which has been handed down to us from
the Christian past is, in one word, the consciousness of
the presence of God.　'My Presence shall go with
thee, and I will give thee rest.'　'The good Hand of
my God upon me' is the Christian's key to the past,
his confidence in the present, his hope for the future.
He looks for no immunity from trouble and sadness,
no exemption from the ills that flesh is heir to.　That
weak and nerveless view of happiness as the mere
negative of pain, or the maximum of possible enjoy-
ment, finds no place in the Christian's outlook.　He
sees in life a struggle, a conflict, a race ; he foresees
many a failure and many a fall, but he knows that in
God's Providence new beginnings are the life of
perseverance, though they seem to contradict it.　And
so he dares to look forward to the future, to turn his
back upon the old and face the new, to forget the
things which are behind and press onward still, in
the knowledge that God is with him.　Under one

condition only will he fear. 'If Thy Presence go not with me, carry me not up hence.' I dare not walk alone without the Presence of my God, whether it be revealed in cloud or fire. Banish that promise of God's Presence, 'Certainly I will be with thee,' and we can understand the sadness, the gloom of life. For it is in that promise that the Christian finds, amid doubt and change and sorrow, his one fixed point, the one constant among many variables.

> 'Change and decay in all around I see,
> O Thou that changest not, abide with me.'

Think what the presence of God in the Christian's life is, how infinitely more it means to us than it could have meant to Moses. To him it meant a signal honour for his people, a separation from all nations by the fact that God was with them, that they were the Lord's host, and God their Captain, their earthly leader only His vicegerent. In the fact of the Incarnation we bow before a greater mystery, we receive a higher gift than patriarch or prophet or Old Testament saint could dream of. In the finished work of God the Son, human life has been transformed. In Holy Baptism we are separated, far more than ever Israel was, separated, not as a nation overshadowed by God's Presence, but as those who, by the grace of union, have been united with God. No outward visible sign of cloud or fire, but the inward reality of a new life, is ours. God and man are no longer separated as they were before Christ came. They are one in Him, 'in Whom dwelleth all

the fulness of the Godhead,' while yet He has taken
our nature upon Him.   And that Presence of God is
ever renewed to us in the Sacrament of love ; when
'we dwell in Christ, and Christ in us, we are one
with Christ, and Christ with us' ; while, if so be that
deadly sin has separated us from that Supernatural
Presence, Christ has Himself ordained and blessed
the ministry of reconciliation, whereby the penitent
is restored to grace.   The whole meaning and purpose of Christianity is to assure to man the Presence
of God, removing that separating barrier which sin
had raised, destroying sin *for* us by the Atonement,
killing down sin *in* us by the power of Divine grace.
Pardon and life are the two needs of man's spiritual
nature, the two gifts of God in Christ, whereby the
Presence of God is secured to us.

But there is a danger in our day that this great
gift of God should be lost to us almost without our
knowing it.   University life is a new beginning.   It
means something of a break with the past.   It synchronises, in the case of most of us, with the first
dawn of intellectual activity ; we are learning to think
for ourselves, and at the moment when we want the
calmest judgment and the coolest head we feel for
the first time in their full strength the special temp-
tations of early manhood ; we are surrounded by a
life which ministers to self-indulgence, and is hostile
to stern moral discipline.   We have learnt perhaps
the A B C of philosophy, and already feel ourselves
competent to make for ourselves our religious creed.
But religion is not made ; it grows, or dies.   A made

religion does not live. Do not misunderstand me. Something of reconstruction must take place in the case of every one who thinks. The faith which we were taught as children, and unhesitatingly received, must become ours in a different sense, if it is to go with us through life. It has to be brought into relation with the new truths of science, of philosophy, of criticism, which are flowing in upon us. We cannot keep it as the only part of our intellectual heritage which must not be examined, hidden away in some sacred place. But it is one thing to try and see the old truths in the light of the new knowledge ; it is another, as it were, to sweep away the old and begin afresh. And this is what men so often do. And before long they discover that the Presence of God, which was with them in the old life, is not with them now. They thought they might drop the practice of religion till they had made a place for it in their new theory of life ; and resume it when the reconstruction was complete. And they find they cannot; though there is still the longing for Him Who made us for Himself, in Whom alone our heart can rest. It is in vain then that they attempt to fill the void with that God to whom the speculative reason, in abstraction from conscience, leads us. No one wants or cares for an abstract First Cause. What the soul needs is a Living God, an invisible personality behind the veil of things we see, who can be to us both a brother in sympathy and a sincere object of worship. ' The only God,' it has been said, ' whom Western Europeans, with a Christian ancestry of a thousand

years behind them, can worship, is the God of
Abraham, Isaac, and Jacob; or rather of S. Paul,
S. Augustine, S. Bernard, and of the innumerable
blessed Saints, canonised or not, who peopled the ages
of Faith.' And religion stands or falls with the belief
in a personal God, and the possibility of communion
with Him. It is from this point then that our reconstruction must start. It is in the light of this truth,
and as an answer to this need alone, that we may
hope to understand the great doctrines of the Trinity
and the Incarnation,—the one the only safeguard of a
real and lasting theism, the other that which renders
possible the union of man with God. All else—Bible,
Creeds, Priesthood, Sacraments—may be left under
God's guiding Hand to find their place in the supernatural life. But once destroy or abandon the belief
in a personal God, one with Whom the soul of man
is in immediate and living contact, and religion ceases
to have a meaning. Is it strange that when the
Presence of God is no longer with us, and within us,
we see nothing but the sadness of life, and are ready
to pray, if prayer were not impossible, 'Carry us not
up hence'?

But why is this unsettlement, this period of reconstruction, necessary? Why can we not simply hold
to the old beliefs of childhood, and leave these dis-
quieting questionings alone? Surely the answer is
that God wills to make our hold on truth, our knowledge of Himself, more real, more true, more
thoroughly our own, than it ever could be if we held
it simply on the authority of another. He seems to

veil His Presence from us for a moment that we may possess Him for ever as our own. Of all real and realised truth we must be able to say, as her fellow-townsmen said to the woman of Samaria, ' Now we believe, not because of thy " speaking " ; for we have heard for ourselves, and know.' We cannot keep our faith and our reason apart. We must in these days have a rational faith, and such a faith implies both a work and a life, an intellectual and a moral effort, energy of will and activity of reason, that it may be able fearlessly to face the facts of life, welcoming and claiming as its own every new discovery as telling us more of Him Who is the Truth, seeing in every change the onward leading of His Hand, Whose Presence gives to life its unity, and its value too.

Do not then, my brothers, when you are called upon to face great questions which touch your religious life, think that the first step in the solution is the discarding of the old truths. The problem for you to solve is not, How am I to invent a new theory of life which shall have in it something corresponding to religion ? but, How am I to carry the old love and trust in God, the old faith in Christ and His Church, out into this new world on which I am entering. It is not courage, but cowardice, to shirk the question, and put another in its place ; it is not intellectual strength, but weakness, to assume without proof that the old and the new are irreconcilable, or that the historic faith of Christendom is not after all the key to modern problems.

II. In the wider life of the Church to which we

belong we are now called upon to face a similar
difficulty. The promise of God's Presence is what it
has always been, 'Lo, I am with you alway, even
unto the end of the world.' But it is impossible to shut
our eyes to the fact that the life of the Church is
entering on a new phase. The old days of protection
are going, if not gone, and men in their little faith
think that religion is going too. A great wave of
secularism seems to be passing over our land, and
beating against the temporal bulwarks of our national
Christianity. And men, good men and true in their
personal relations with God, men who have learned to
see His Presence and His Hand in all the changes of
their own lives, are getting anxious and doubtful, or
desponding, as if God's promise to His Church had
failed. Their state is closely parallel to that of men
who feel the old faith, as they learned it at their
mother's knee, falling away from them, who see the
new truths which have yet to be brought into relation
with the old, and have not the heart to face the
problem. So either they shut their eyes to it, and
retreat into the fastnesses of faith, or abandon almost
petulantly the old supernatural creed as if it were
now outgrown.

And yet if, in the retrospect of the individual life,
new beginnings are seen to be the life of perseverance
for those who have the courage to persevere, a retrospect of the Church's history abundantly proves
the same truths. May it not be that in this state of
transition and reconstruction in which we are called
to play our parts, the life of the English Church is

adapting itself, as it has done again and again, to changed circumstances? At least we have no right to assume that a new beginning means that the old was false, that we must seek a new Presence to go with us in the days that are to come.

There are those who vivaciously tell us that it is so ; men, who in what they consider to be the discrediting of the faith of the Church, see the beginning of that earthly millennium when everybody will agree with everybody else, because nobody will believe anything in particular ; when we shall all recognise the indefeasible right of the individual soul to commit spiritual suicide, and the intolerance of seeking to prevent it ; when we shall be bound together in a universal brotherhood, on the basis, not of a common faith, but of a common rejection of the Creed of Christendom.

The experience of the past, however, gives us little confidence in this modern programme. Its all-embracing unity is a delusion, for there is no lasting bond of cohesion among those who find themselves together on the negative side of a dichotomous division. As long as Protestantism meant, what it did mean in England in the Reformation period, a positive body of definite beliefs, distinguished alike from Popery on the one side and Puritanism on the other, it had power and vitality and unity ; but when it was extended to include, as it includes to-day, all the 220 sects who reject the Papal claims, it has ceased to have any meaning at all.

Nor can we get real moral strength out of so vague

a faith. At least in the past, power and definiteness have been strangely associated together. We are a practical people, and we rightly judge a religion, not by the satisfaction it brings to the speculative reason, but by the power it exercises over the moral life. But when the conception of God is evacuated of all it means to the Christian consciousness, and 'defecated to an abstraction,' it is emptied also of its power. Try it, if you dare, in the hour of strong temptation, when the enemy is coming in like a flood, and your foot is almost gone. Try, and you will know in a moment that the powers of evil owe neither allegiance nor reverence to the modern substitute for the Christian's God. 'Jesus I know, and Paul I know, but who are ye?' No, there is no moral strength in a generalised religion. A faith which is invented to suit everybody will have the power to help nobody.

It may be that we shall live to see the truth of Christ's Holy Church put on a level with all religions and no religions. We may live to see the dis-establishment of the Church of S. Augustine, and the alienation of the material wealth which by the piety of founders and benefactors was dedicated to God for ever. If this be God's will, it is for His glory and our good. But such changes cannot touch the promise of His Presence given to the Church for ever. Only if the Church itself is false to her great trust will that Presence of God be withdrawn. If she allows herself to speak and think, as some of her members do, as if the Divine mission of the Church were dependent on the accidents of the Church's life; only if she allows herself to believe that a new beginning is a confession that her faith is vain, and seeks to put some human invention in the place of the truth in God ; only if she presumes to make terms with the world she was bidden to overcome,—only then, will the Presence of God be lost to her, and the promise made of none effect. It is because the Church has faith in God, faith in His unfailing promise, faith in His working, however weak may seem the instruments He uses, faith in His Presence in her and above her, that, come what may, she dares to thank Him and to go forward.

And here there is much to encourage us in a retrospect of the past. I look back over three centuries and a half, and I see a noble and vigorous effort, on the part of our English Church, to shake off the tyranny of a foreign power, and to purify the faith she had received from the Apostles. And even as we watch our Church making that glorious effort to be pure and free, a torrent of foreign heresy pours in,—false teaching which, under the disguise of purity and truth, would destroy both faith and morals, the Church, the Bible, the Priesthood, the Sacraments, nay, with its revived Arianism, would deny the very Lord that bought us. Put yourselves back into the feelings of a Churchman in the sixteenth century, one who loved, and honoured, and believed in the historical faith of England. What is he to do? Accept the Roman view and abandon his faith in the Church of his baptism ? or wait and see all faith swept away by the advancing tide of Zwinglianism and Calvinism and Anabaptism? Could we have wondered if hopelessly he had cried out, ' Lord, take away my life ; I only am left.'   And yet the faith has outlived its foes, and come forth from that period of transition with a stronger hold on the conscience and the morals of the people.

One who has spent the best years of his life in the study of that troubled period of our Church's history, and himself looks back with something of regret to the old order that then passed away, yet gives no uncertain sound as to the Churchman's duty at such a time : ' When life is ebbing, and the advent of a new existence is at hand advancing as noiselessly and yet as certain as the dawn, blandly tolerant of our small cares and griefs as it sweeps along, but not the less to be diverted from its benevolent and irresistible course, we are apt to think that its progress might have been stayed had our wisdom devised different measures and adopted in due time other remedies than those on which we relied.   So it is with the death and the new birth of the world.   We mistake its causes, we misread its meaning.   True love, and not less wise than true, will shed a tear, and strew the grave with flowers : then turning its face to the grey and shivering dawn, bind up its loins for the new race, though different to our seeming, not less full of life, not less divine, than that which has passed irrevocably away.'[1]

' Not less full of life, not less divine,' and yet so different from what has been.   Can we believe this of that new phase on which the Church is entering in these last days?   Forty years ago it was

[1] Brewer's *Reign of Henry VIII.*, vol. i. p. 580.

possible for Dr. Newman to say of the Church of England, 'O my Mother! who hath put this note upon thee, to have a miscarrying womb and dry breasts, to be strange to thine own flesh, and thine eye cruel to thy little ones?' Could he, if he were still with us, use such words now? And yet, one by one, the Church is being shorn of her privileges, encroached on by State Courts, assailed by treachery within and foes without, and in spite of all, 'not less full of life, not less divine,' not less indwelt by the Presence of her God, she has gone forward, has dared to face the grey and shivering dawn, her faith strong in the promise of her Lord, and the loyalty of her children.

'Not less full of life, not less divine.' Is our faith strong enough to believe and to act? For here in our little world of Oxford we have a battle to fight and win. It is easy to look back sadly to the Oxford that has been. It is easy to throw up the hands as if all were lost. But the mission of the Church in Oxford is not at an end because she can no longer claim it as exclusively her own; because she has no longer the protection which once walled her round and enabled her to live at ease; because in some sense she must make a new beginning and justify her right to exist. The promised Presence is not withdrawn because the Church which in the old days so often failed in her duty to the nation has lost her ancient rights. She is calling on her true sons to follow her as she goes forth, 'not less full of life, not less divine,' than in the ancient days, to face once more the grey and

shivering dawn, till it grows bright with the radiancy
of her children's faith, and the full sunlight of her God.

In the controversies of the Church in every age, as
in the struggles of our own individual lives, it is im-
patience that leads men from the truth. We are
tempted to a reckless abandonment of eternal
principles because in their traditional setting they
do not fit the present need.

But you cannot make a new religion. It is not by
abandoning the Christian faith, but by being true to
the faith we hold, that we shall reach the religion of
the future. Amidst all the changes of the sixteenth
century, when the Church was driven from the shade
of the monastery to the broad daylight of the world,
not one article of Christian faith was lost or left behind. And if we are to judge the future by the past,
those whom God will choose to guide His Church
through the crisis of the present age will be neither
men who, panic-struck and despairing, shrink from
change, nor those who recklessly abandon the ancient
faith for some nineteenth-century *nostrum*, but real men,
who being not like children carried away with every
' blast of vain doctrine,' have the strength to face the
problem. It will be those who, in all the changes and
struggles of their own spiritual lives, can trace the
guiding Hand of God, and therefore in the wider
issues of the Church at large are strong enough to
rest and wait, ready to face the grey and shivering
dawn of a new era, yet true to the ancient Christian
faith and strong in the promised Presence of their
God.

# VI.

## DECISION FOR GOD.[1]

*'Choose you this day whom ye will serve.'*—JOSHUA xxiv. 15.

IT was the farewell charge of the veteran chieftain Joshua to the tribes of Israel gathered together at Shechem. He had watched the childhood of the nation. He had seen a band of fugitives organised into an army, disciplined by adversity, entering at last as a victorious nation on the promised possession. He had watched their religious history, the triumph of the great truth of the One God which they were to hold as a sacred deposit, and hand down to after ages. It was their greatness that to them were committed 'the oracles of God.' Yet he had seen them already false to their high mission. He had noted the reappearance of polytheistic ideas, he had seen the return to the Apis-worship of Egypt, he had mourned over the importation of more than one foreign cult. He knew that he was the leader of a chosen people, but of a people chosen not for their own greatness, but for a special duty or vocation in God's world. And he saw that they had not realised their vocation. In the new phase of their history on which they were entering, everything now turned

[1] Preached to Undergraduates at S. Mary's, Oxford, Feb. 7, 1886.

upon a choice. They were at a solemn crisis. God
had chosen them for His work: but God's choice
is never absolute, never a mere selection for pre-
eminence, never a mere display of power, but part of
a great purpose which runs through time. To fail to
do that work to which God calls is, by that failure, to
nullify the choice. It was then a matter of life and
death for Israel. How would they decide?

And the place in which that question should
be asked and answered was full of memories. It
was there, tradition said, that the first promise had
been made to Abraham: 'Unto thy seed will I give
this land.'[1] It was there, at Shechem, that the
patriarch Jacob had purged his house of idols[2] and
restored the worship of the One True God. It was
there, in the valley between Ebal and Gerizim, the
mount of cursing and the mount of blessing, that in
obedience to the word of Moses the Law had been
rehearsed. It was there that the embalmed body of
Joseph, which they had brought from Egypt, was to
find its final resting-place. Such were the associations which gathered round them as the multitudes
in the valley of decision listened to the words of the
great Ephraimite leader, and the charge was a retrospect and a prospect, a review of God's unchanging
goodness, and an anxious, doubtful looking forward
to the future. Would the people be true to their
mission? God had given them a land for which they
did not labour: He had driven out the nations before
them. But for what? 'That they might keep His

[1] Gen. xii. 7.          [2] Gen. xxxv. 1-4.

statutes and observe His laws,' that they might be the repositories of the great truth which was to prepare the world for its regeneration, the truth of monotheism, which should prepare for Christianity. Would they be true to their vocation? Had they really apprehended that for which they had been apprehended? Would they choose that for which God had chosen them? If not, still they must choose. 'If it seem evil unto you to serve the Lord, choose you this day whom ye will serve.' Shall it be the polytheism from which Abraham had been called, or the polytheism of the Amorites among whom they now dwelt? They might choose their vocation to be the servants of the One True God, or they might choose among the many idolatries in which they might miss their vocation. But choose they must.

But for himself, the aged leader, the choice was made. His trumpet had not given an uncertain sound; he had not swerved from his allegiance to the God of Abraham; he was too old to reconsider his position. He might almost have adopted the words of a great Christian martyr.[1] The God that he had served all his life long he had found true. 'As for me and my house, we will serve the Lord.'

It was not strange that in such surroundings and at such a time the enthusiasm of faith should communicate itself to the people. All the idolatry and rebellion against God was forgotten. It seemed so impossible to hesitate. God forbid that we should forsake the Lord to serve other gods. Yes! He was

[1] Cf. *The Martyrdom of S. Polycarp*, § 9.

K

a holy and a jealous God.   He would not share His
Throne.   They knew that before Joshua told them,
yet with impulsive self-confidence they cry: 'Nay,
but we will serve the Lord.   The Lord our God will
we serve, and His Voice will we obey.'   They made
their choice.

From Shechem to Mount Carmel it was no great
distance.   But the scene has changed.   Five hundred
years have rolled by since Joshua died.   Two rival
altars are there.   Around the one is a crowd of
priests, exhausted with their fanatical imprecations
and savage self-mutilation ; before the other stands the
Prophet of the God of Abraham.   It is a tremendous
issue, an awful moment of choice.   ' How long halt ye
between two opinions ?   If the Lord be God, follow
Him ; but if Baal, then follow him.'   How different
from the appeal of Joshua !   There is no mention
now of God's great mercies in the past ; no appeal to
the allegiance which, by the worship of Baal, they
had renounced ; only the silent reproach of Elijah as
' he repaired the altar of the Lord, which was broken
down ' ;   only the irresistible associations which
gathered round them as ' the time of the offering of
evening sacrifice ' drew near.   It was like the sound
of some far-off church bell borne to the sinner's ears
even in the act of sin.   A great revelation of power
is to be given.   'The God that answereth by fire, let
him be God.'   Elijah, 'faithful among the faithless
found,' stands alone over against the many Baal
priests ; the people in awestruck silence wait for the
result.   They have lost their faith, but they will side

with the stronger, with the God that can prove His
right to their allegiance. And the mountains are
hushed to the Lord's controversy, till, as the fire
descends, they echo with the shout : 'The Lord, He
is the God ! the Lord, He is the God !' But souls
are rarely won by an act of power. It was not
among the crowd of Baal-worshippers who professed
'instantaneous conversion' that the truth of God
lived on ; it was in the steadfastness of the faithful
prophet and of the seven thousand men who had not
bowed the knee to Baal, and needed no miracle to
restore their faith.

Let us look at one more scene in the history of the
chosen people. Two centuries after the miracle on
Mount Carmel the northern kingdom was carried
into captivity. The kingdom of Judah was spared a
little longer, and then they too were torn from their
native land. Then came the days of the Captivity
and the return of the remnant, the building of the
Temple and the restoration of its worship, and all
the dreary story of the life of the Jews of Palestine
under their successive conquerors. Four hundred
years have passed since Malachi sealed the book of
the prophets. A voice had come from the desert
summoning to repentance, and a new Teacher, Who
spake as never man spake, and loved as only God
can love, had gone in and out amongst the people,
had healed the sick, and taught the ignorant, and
raised the weak, and held out the helping hand to
the sinner and the fallen, while He sternly rebuked the
pride and unreality and self-seeking of those who sat

in Moses' seat. And the forces of envy and hate have gathered round that gentle, loving life, and the crowds are thronging in the streets of the Holy City to claim their privilege, and Pilate, the representative of the hated power of Rome, has bidden them to use their right and make their choice. 'Whom will ye that I release unto you, Barabbas or Jesus, Which is called Christ?' And the answer came: 'Not this man, but Barabbas.' What then shall be done with Jesus? 'And they cried aloud, Let Him be crucified!' And these were the children of the men who had declared for God at Shechem: 'Nay, but we will serve the Lord. The Lord our God will we serve, and His Voice will we obey.' The climax of national apostasy was reached when they put the Messiah to death. Surely they did not know, they could not have known, that Christ was the Son of God, even that He was the fulfilment of their Messianic hope! No, they did not know. But they knew that He Whom they crucified was one who reproved their lives, and they hated the Light because their deeds were evil.

It would seem at first as if, whatever may have been the case with the chosen people, such tremendous moments do not come to us ; at least, if they did, we think we should not hesitate to choose the right : God, not Baal, Jesus, not Barabbas. Put before a man the broad antithesis, God and the devil, heaven and hell, or, in morals, virtue and vice, sensuality and self-denial, and he would not stay to deliberate. Only a Miltonic devil could say, 'Evil, be thou my good.' No one chooses evil as evil.

Our difficulties arise from the confusion of the spheres of good and evil; in particular cases the devil comes to us not as a devil, but disguised as an angel of light, and we are deceived. We find we have decided some momentous issue without knowing how great the issue was.

Yes, and hundreds and hundreds who are now living vicious and godless lives might say the same. 'We never remember having a great choice put before us.' No, it is not by the first choice, a choice made once for all, that character is formed, but by a series of acts of choice which test our loyalty to God and goodness.

'Take the first turning to the right, and keep straight on,' said Bishop Wilberforce to some navvies who half in ridicule had asked him if he could tell them the way to Heaven. But it is *the keeping straight on* which is the difficulty, not the first turning to the right. Every step in moral progress, every advance in spiritual knowledge, implies a new act of will, a new effort after good, so that the very existence of moral and spiritual life in us depends on choice, *decision for God*—not once and for all, but constantly through life. But we do not like to have to choose. It has almost come to be thought a proof of higher wisdom to suspend our judgment, to live in an atmosphere of serene indifference, and condescendingly to say of those great questions, which trouble more earnest and nobler souls, that there is probably a good deal to be said on both sides.

That is true of many, perhaps most, speculative

questions ; it is true of matters which depend upon experience. It is *not* true of questions in morals and religion. There we cannot escape decision. To suspend our judgment there is to decide *against* the higher truth. We can drift into vice, as we can drift into unbelief, but a real faith and a real holiness implies the active use of powers which God has given us.

It will not come to us then, that moment of choice, as a great contrast between virtue and vice, a clear antithesis between God and Baal—yet the antithesis is implicit. We have to choose between a higher and a lower, a more and a less right, a harder and an easier way. It does not look like a great crisis ; we think it cannot matter much. And yet our conscience is strangely sensitive about it. It whispers to us that there, behind the mist, are the opposing heights of Ebal and Gerizim. The choice we have to make is between life and death, God and the devil, heaven and hell. We are to choose whom we will serve. Not to choose is to choose amiss.

Every choice, says the great German philosopher-poet, is for eternity. Yet men realise that often only when it is too late. They have let everything go by default. They were in theory Christians ; they imagined they had taken sides, had chosen Him Who in Holy Baptism chose them. But, when the moment of choice comes, when the temptation is at hand, they shrink from the effort of decision for God, and they give way to evil. Then the momentum of that false choice carries them further. It is not merely that, by the law of habit, acts tend to reproduce themselves. That is true, and it is true of good as well as evil acts. But every choice has a twofold consequence. It reacts upon the *conscience* and it reacts upon the *will*. To choose the higher is to give definiteness and precision and a diviner insight to the *conscience*, even while it gives to the *will* new power to be free. But the *conscience*, once silenced, speaks in a lower tone, judges less certainly and less truly; and the *will*, in that its wilfulness opposed itself and chose the lower line, is weaker by the act, and has so far lost its freedom. For the freedom of the will, which we vaguely talk about, is a freedom to be *won*; the divine light of conscience is at first a spark that may be quenched or kindled. The perfect freedom that can choose God, the perfect light that reveals Him,—these belong only to the Perfect Man 'Who knew no sin.'

Our whole moral and spiritual life consists in the use we make of the power of choice in little things. It is here, in what seem petty skirmishes, not in great engagements, that the battle is won or lost. Make the little acts of life matters of conscience—the line we take up, the friendships we form, the amusements we take part in—all these, so far as they are matters of choice, have their bearing upon the great question of life—nay, are themselves but new ways in which that question is being answered: 'He that is faithful in that which is least is faithful also in much; and he that is unjust in the least, is unjust also in much.'— To follow the line of least resistance, to do that which requires the smallest effort, to be content with a minimum—all these are signs of a weak will and a half-silenced conscience. I am afraid there are many among us whose main object in life is to avoid the responsibility or the effort of choice. They would rather not commit themselves—that is the phrase. So they adopt a *laisser faire* attitude. They do not see that haziness on the great questions of morals and religion is not a proof of strength but of indolence. I do not of course mean that great questions of truth and falsehood, right and wrong, can be settled off-hand by an act of will. I mean that to cultivate decision of character, and always, in questions however trifling, to decide in favour of the higher, is to make the solution of those questions possible. ' If I could only believe your creed,' a dissolute youth once said to Pascal, 'I should be a better man.' ' Begin,' said Pascal, 'by being a better man, and you may come to believe in my creed.'

Every act of moral choice is a choosing or rejecting of God, and makes more possible or less possible the knowledge of His truth. ' Choose ye this day whom ye will serve' applies therefore not only to those who are halting between two opinions, but to those who have taken the side of God, and at every moment of their lives are being challenged to make good their choice. Only remember He chose you before He called upon you to choose Him. In Baptism He laid His hand upon you, in Confirmation He sealed you, in the the Holy Eucharist He gave Himself to you. Man's power of choice, like his knowledge of moral truth, is God's primal gift. For us Christians it has been renewed and strengthened by union with His perfect humanity, that we may freely choose His Service Whose Love has chosen us.

See then that ye walk worthy of the vocation wherewith ye are called. You are born to be free ; no power but your own can make you slaves. You are born to know God ; only your own acts can blind your eyes to the truth. God calls upon you to use the powers that He has given you to choose His Service, Who has made you free.

You are entering upon a new year, are you strong enough for the life of moral effort ? Will you dare, in days when every eye is on those who have the courage of their opinions, to say that you have made your choice and will abide by it ; that come what may, you mean to act up to all the light and truth which God has given you ; that you are not ashamed to declare yourself the servant of Him Whose Love we celebrate at Christmas-tide ?

Do not be a crypto-Christian, like him who came to Jesus by night. You do not know how many younger men may be looking up to you, waiting for a hint from you that you have chosen Christ. It is a cruel wrong to them, as it is a grievous hurt to yourself. For it is on what seem uneventful skirmishes that the victory for God is lost or won. It is of particular acts that character is formed. It is by the little decisions of daily life that the choice is made, the choice which is for ever.

Printed by T. and A. CONSTABLE, Printers to Her Majesty, at the Edinburgh University Press.